AF773409

CONCEPTS IN LAW

In a componential analysis of meaning, there are usually several conditions which do not use the words of which the meanings are specified. Examples would be 'The sentence "It is raining" means that (is true if and only if) there are drops of water falling down from the sky, caused by condensation in the clouds', and 'The word "dog" stands for (is applicable to) four-legged domesticated animals that bark'. Associated with componential analyses is the idea of meaning rules. These rules, which govern the meanings of words and, indirectly, of sentences, specify the criteria for the use of words and the truth conditions of sentences. A componential analysis of meaning has the advantage that it is useful to instruct the meanings of words and sentences and to make understandable how somebody who knows the meaning of a word or sentence, is capable to use this word or sentence correctly.

An important thing to notice about componential analyses is that they make word meanings perform two functions at the same time. On the one hand these meanings bring about a coupling between a word and the 'things' denoted by it, and on the other hand they demarcate the boundaries of this category of things. In schema (Fig. 4):

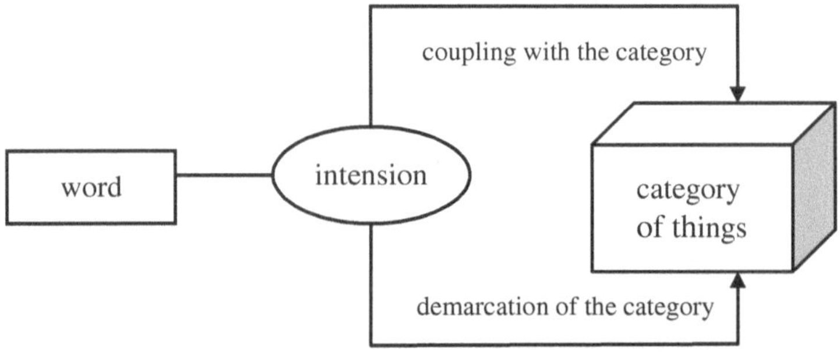

Fig. 4

The above examples of componential analyses of meaning may not be convincing. Although this may be caused by a lack of imagination of the author, I take it that something more serious is at stake. In my opinion, a componential analysis only makes sense in case of words and sentences with artificially assigned meanings, based on stipulative definitions, such as 'laser' or – in the legal sphere – 'obligation'. Although a speaker of a language normally can recognise instances of a word's denotation, he does not know precise criteria by means of which these instances can be identified, let alone that he knows the precise criteria that give the word's meaning. Most people know how to recognise normal dogs under normal circumstances, but they do not know any criteria specifying the meaning of the word 'dog' and not even criteria by means of which they usually recognise dogs.[15] Apparently it is possible to know the meaning of a word or sentence without

[15] This issue is discussed more extensively in J.C. Hage, *Feiten en betekenis* (Facts and meaning), Ph.D.-thesis, Leiden 1987, Chapter IV (in Dutch).

CONCEPTS IN LAW

Edited by

JAAP C. HAGE
University of Maastricht,
The Netherlands

DIETMAR VON DER PFORDTEN
University of Göttingen,
Germany

Springer

Editors
Prof. Jaap C. Hage
University of Maastricht
Dept. Metajuridica
6200 MD Maastricht
Netherlands
jaap.hage@maastrichtuniversity.nl

Prof. Dietmar von der Pfordten
Universität Göttingen
Platz der Göttinger Sieben 6
37073 Göttingen
Germany
dpfordt@gwdg.de

ISSN 1572-4395
ISBN 978-90-481-2981-2 e-ISBN 978-90-481-2982-9
DOI 10.1007/978-90-481-2982-9
Springer Dordrecht Heidelberg London New York

Library of Congress Control Number: 2009929296

© Springer Science+Business Media B.V. 2009
No part of this work may be reproduced, stored in a retrieval system, or transmitted in any form or by any means, electronic, mechanical, photocopying, microfilming, recording or otherwise, without written permission from the Publisher, with the exception of any material supplied specifically for the purpose of being entered and executed on a computer system, for exclusive use by the purchaser of the work.

Printed on acid-free paper

Springer is part of Springer Science+Business Media (www.springer.com)

Contents

About the Authors

Åke Frändberg (e-mail: Ake.Frandberg@jur.uu.se) is emeritus professor of Jurisprudence at Uppsala University, Sweden. Among his publications can be mentioned the books *Om analog användning av rättsnormer* (On Analogical Use of Legal Norms, 1973), *Rättsregel och rättsval* (The Concept Legal Rule and Choices of Law, 1984) and *Rättsordningens idé* (The Idea of Legal Order, 2005).

His main interests are the investigation of general legal concepts and the interpretation and application of law. His present research is focused on the idea of the Law-State (*Rechtsstaat*, the Rule of Law).

Jaap Hage (e-mail: jaap.hage@maastrichtuniversity.nl) holds the chair of Jurisprudence at the University of Maastricht in the Netherlands. His earlier publications include the books *Reasoning with Rules* (Dordrecht 1997) and *Studies in Legal Logic* (Dordrecht 2005).

His present research focuses on general legal concepts and on the method of legal science.

Lorenz Kähler (e-mail: lkaehler@web.de) works at the chair of Philosophy of Law and Social Philosophy at the University of Göttingen, Germany. He has published on overruling decisions.

Currently, he writes about the concept and characteristics of default rules.

Dennis Patterson (e-mail: dpatters@camden.rutgers.edu) holds the Chair in Legal Theory and Legal Philosophy at the European University Institute in Florence. He is Board of Governors Professor of Law and Philosophy at Rutgers University School of Law (Camden) and he holds a Chair in Jurisprudence and International Trade at Swansea school of Law, UK. His most recent book is *The New Global Trading Order* (with Ari Afilalo; Cambridge 2008).

Dietmar von der Pfordten (e-mail: dpfordt@gwdg.de) holds the chair of Philosophy of Law and Social Philosophy at the University of Göttingen in Germany. His earlier publications include the books *Deskription, Evaluation und Präskription* (Berlin 1993), *Ökologische Ethik* (Reinbek 1996), *Rechtsethik* (Munich 2001) and *Normative Ethik* (forthcoming 2010).

His research focuses on practical philosophy and philosophy of law.

Ralf Poscher (e-mail: poscher@poscher.eu) holds the chair of Public Law, Sociology and Philosophy of Law at the Ruhr-University Bochum in Germany. His publications focus on constitutional law and legal theory. Presently he works on theoretical questions of adjudication.

Giovanni Sartor (e-mail: giovanni.sartor@eui.eu) is professor of Legal Informatics and Legal Theory at the European University Institute of Florence and at the University of Bologna. His publications include the book *Legal Reasoning: A Cognitive Approach to the Law* (Dordrecht 2005).

His current research focuses on logical models of legal knowledge and legal reasoning, on game theory and the law, and on ICT in the legislative process.

Torben Spaak (e-mail: Torben.Spaak@jur.uu.se) is professor in jurisprudence at the Department of Law, Uppsala University, where he teaches jurisprudence and legal reasoning. He has published two monographs in core areas of jurisprudence, and a number of articles on jurisprudential topics in international journals of law, jurisprudence, or philosophy, such as *Buffalo Human Rights Law Review*, *Ratio Juris*, *Law and Philosophy*, *Analisi e diritto*, *Archiv für Rechts- und Sozialphilosophie*, and *Theoria*.

Contributors

Åke Frändberg Uppsala University, Uppsala, Sweden, Ake.Frandberg@jur.uu.se

Jaap Hage University of Maastricht, Maastricht, Netherlands, jaap.hage@maastrichtuniversity.nl

Lorenz Kähler University of Göttingen, Göttingen, Germany, lkaehler@web.de

Dennis Patterson Rutgers University School of Law, Camden, US, dpatters@camden.rutgers.edu

Dietmar von der Pfordten University of Göttingen, Göttingen, Germany, dpfordt@gwdg.de

Ralf Poscher Ruhr-University Bochum, Bochum, Germany, poscher@poscher.eu

Giovanni Sartor European University Institute of Florence, Florence, Italy, giovanni.sartor@eui.eu

Torben Spaak Department of Law, Uppsala University, Uppsala, Sweden, Torben.Spaak@jur.uu.se

Introduction

Concepts play a central role in the law, because all forms of law are formulated with the help of terms that express – in the eyes of many at least – concepts. Concepts are also important in the study of law's nature in philosophy of law and legal theory. After some decades of neglect, concepts are nowadays rediscovered by general philosophy, epistemology, cognitive science, psychology, artificial intelligence, informatics and – this is at least one of our aims in editing this volume – also philosophy of law and legal theory.

This crucial role of concepts in the law and their recent rediscovery by several disciplines were the reasons to organise a special workshop on concepts in the law during the conference of the International Society of Philosophy of Law and Social Philosophy (IVR) 2007 in Cracow. A selection of the papers presented at this workshop is collected in this volume. The topics of the selected papers provide an illuminating overview of the different ways in which concepts are involved in the law and the philosophical and theoretical analysis of the law.

The first paper in this volume, *An Essay on Legal Concept Formation*, by Åke Frändberg is introductory and methodological by nature. It consists essentially of a number of distinctions between the many functions concepts play in the law. The basic difference pointed out by Frändberg is between the juridical-operative function and the law-stating function of concepts. To state it overly simple, concepts in the juridical-operative function are used to deal with the law while concepts in the law-stating function are the concepts used in legal norms. One of the editors of this collection experienced the practical relevance of this basic distinction when he wanted to present an analysis of legal transactions in general, while part of his audience expected an exposition of the rules that specify when a legal transaction is valid. In the terminology of Frändberg, he wanted to analyse legal transactions in their juridical-operative function, while the audience expected a discussion of legal transactions in their law-stating function. Apart from this basic distinction, Frändberg makes a number of other relevant distinctions that are very helpful to avoid confusions about the roles of concepts in the law.

Also the second paper in this volume, *About Concepts in Law,* by Dietmar von der Pfordten is introductory by nature. Von der Pfordten starts by attacking 'normativism', that is the today widely accepted view in legal theory that norms (rules, principles) play the primary role in the law, and not, for instance, concepts or institutions. Von der Pfordten first discusses the nature of concepts and of conceptual analysis in general. Second he investigates the way in which concepts are related in a conceptual scheme. He then returns to the law and answers the question how these general findings can be applied to legal conceptualisation. Especially interesting in this discussion is a fourfold division between the levels of abstraction of concepts, and its relevance for the issue to what extent general concepts are malleable by the law. Von der Pfordten argues that in particular those concepts which are one level more or one level less abstract than the concepts that function on the level of perception are most malleable by the law. By way of conclusion, he returns to the question whether normativism is correct. Von der Pfordten argues that normativism neglects the central and independent role of concepts in legal reasoning. He therefore rejects the view of Alf Ross, who held in his famous paper *Tû-Tû* that the meanings of intermediate legal concepts, such as 'owner' could be reduced to the norms that specify when they are applicable and the norms that specify the consequences of their applicability.

Alf Ross' Tû-Tû paper also plays an important role in the contributions of Giovanni Sartor and Jaap Hage. Giovanni Sartor starts the third paper in this volume, *Understanding and Applying Legal Concepts: An Inquiry on Inferential Meaning*, with the observation that Ross' analysis of the meaning of intermediate legal concepts was in one important respect correct: the meanings of these concepts can indeed be specified in terms of the roles they play in legal argument chains, on the basis of the rules that specify when they are applicable and the consequences of their applicability. From this observation he draws the conclusion that at least for these concepts there is no demarcation between on the one hand their meanings and on the other hand the positive law that specifies their roles in the legal system.

But then a problem arises. Does understanding an intermediate legal concept imply that one endorses the corresponding contents of the law? Suppose that a legal system uses the concept of a patriarchal marriage. The meaning of this concept is given by the following rules:

> *IF* a couple goes through a marriage ceremony, *THEN* the two spouses are in the relation of patriarchal marriage,

and

> *IF* two spouses are in the relation of patriarchal marriage, *THEN* the husband has power over his wife.

Does one's knowledge of the meaning of term *patriarchal marriage* commit one to the view that whenever a couple has gone through a marriage ceremony, the husband has power over his wife? This is not a position that Sartor wants to adopt. To avoid it, he devotes the second part of his paper to an analysis of inferential meaning that does not commit a person who knows the inferential meaning of a concept to endorsement of the rules that define this meaning. To this purpose he makes use of a technique developed by Ramsey to replace intermediate concepts by an existentially quantified variable and a technique developed by Carnap to distinguish between the possession (understanding) of a concept and its endorsement.

In the fourth paper in this collection, *The Meaning of Legal Status Words*, Jaap Hage also takes the analysis of Alf Ross as his starting point, but focuses on Ross' claim that words like 'owner' do not have a proper meaning, because their sole role is to function as intermediaries in legal argument chains. First Hage argues that words like 'owner' do, opposite to what Ross argued, denote entities. To be sure, these entities do not exist in physical reality, but next to the physical reality there is a social reality in which entities can exist because their existence follows from the application of rules. Words such as 'owner' denote a legal status which exists in the rule-based (institutionalised) part of social reality. There are rules which specify when such a status comes into being or ends, and what the consequences of its presence are.

The next question is whether these rules specify the meanings of legal status words. Here Hage takes a fundamentally different position than Sartor. According to Hage, the rules that govern the use of legal status words do *not* specify their meanings. The meaning of a word like 'owner' is that it stands for owners, nothing more. Are the rules irrelevant for the meanings of legal status words, then? No, their importance lies in the fact that one should know about these rules to know what the legal status for which they stand involves. Without knowing the rules that govern ownership, one does not know what ownership is. And if one does not know what ownership is, one does not know what the word 'owner' means either. But from this it does not follow that the rules governing the use of legal status words specify their meanings.

One legal concept that is mostly used in a juridical-operative function is the concept of a power or competence. (Hart, however, has created the impression that it is commonly used in a law-stating function, by writing about 'power conferring rules'). In the fifth paper in this collection, *Explicating the Concept of Legal Competence*, Torben Spaak offers an extensive analysis of this concept and of what the exercise of a competence is. He connects competence conceptually with changes in legal positions that are brought about by acts which then count as exercises of competence:

> A person, *p*, has the competence in regard to a legal position, *LP*, if, and only if, there is a competence-exercising-act, *a*, such that it depends for its legal effect on having been performed with an (actual or imputed) intent to bring about the relevant legal effect, and a situation, *S*, such that if *p* in *S* performs *a*, and thus goes about it in the right way, *p* will, through *a*, change *LP*.

Apart from this analysis, Spaak discusses a number of subdivisions between types of competence, the most common being that between autonomous and heteronomous competence.

When concepts are used in their law-stating function, they become the object of legal manipulation. By broadening or narrowing a concept's scope of application, the contents of the law can be changed. This well-known phenomenon is at the focus of the contributions by Lorenz Kähler and Ralf Poscher, be it that they approach it with different purposes in mind. Kähler raises in his contribution *Do Normative Reasons Completely Determine the Formation of Legal Concepts?* the questions whether the normative character of the law completely explains which concepts are used and which meanings they have, or whether there are other aspects which determine their content. That there is such an influence is, at first glance, obvious. But it is less obvious what exactly it consists in. If legal concepts have an objective 'deep structure', as Dworkin argues, they might not be open to an unlimited manipulation according to one's moral or ideological agenda. Kähler argues that there are several independent ways in which normative considerations can influence the choice and definition of legal concepts but that there are also constraints on this influence. These constraints date back to the functions legal concepts must fulfil. Legal concepts must be used in various contexts and express different states of affairs, the evaluation of which might differ.

In the seventh paper in this volume, *The Hand of Midas. When Concepts Turn Legal, or Deflating the Hart-Dworkin Debate*, Ralf Poscher also takes the malleability of legal concepts as his starting point, but uses it as a stepping point for understanding the relation between law and morality. As soon as a concept is used in stating the law, the precise scope of application of this concept has become a legal matter. This is what Poscher calls 'The Midas Quality of the Law'. Just as everything that was touched by the legendary King Midas turned into gold, everything that is touched by the law becomes legal. This also holds for concepts with a moral import. When these concepts are used in a law stating function, they receive a specifically legal content. In the words of Poscher: 'The law and morality only share common concepts but not common conceptions.' Based on this observation, Poscher argues that the Hart-Dworkin debate is based on a wrong presupposition, namely that the use of common concepts implies that moral conceptions of these concepts would be legally relevant as such and not only as one source amongst others out of which the specifically legal conceptions are developed.

The question whether legal concepts are defined by means of the rules that specify their roles in legal arguments presupposes that the concepts are used in their law-stating function. The final paper in this volume, written by Dennis Patterson, focuses on the other main function of legal concepts, that is their juridical-operative function. One feature of this function is to provide a perspective on the law as a whole. Is the law, for instance, depicted as a set of norms that guide action, or as a set of protected interests? That concepts used in their law-stating function influence the contents of the law is obvious. Less obvious, at least nowadays, is that the concept of law determines this content too. Dworkin deserves the honour of having placed this role of the concept, or – maybe better – the conceptions of law on the legal philosophical agenda again. Our conception of the law may influence our position on what the law is in particular cases. It is somewhat ironic to notice that this makes analysis of the concept of law – the kind of work that Hart undertook in his major study, and which was criticised by Dworkin – relevant for the contents of the law in particular cases.

There is a major difference, however, between the styles of analysis proposed by Hart and Dworkin, at least according to Dennis Patterson in the eighth contribution to this volume, *After Conceptual Analysis: The Rise of Practice Theory*. Where Hart would take the practice of the participants in the law as defining the concept of law, for Dworkin this would merely be the starting point of a theoretical analysis. In contrast to Dworkin, Hart would hold a 'practice theory' of the law. Under a practice theory Patterson understands 'an account of the law that answers the question "What is the law in this jurisdiction with respect to x?" by looking at how participants in the practice decide the state of the law'.

This raises the question what a practice is, and Patterson devotes the second half of his contribution to the analysis of practice and practice theory. To this purpose he refers to a study by Rouse which offers an account of practice theory at the hand of six themes. According to Patterson, the goal of any practice theory of law is to make sense of the practice as an ongoing, iterative and common activity. The normativity of the law is in this connection the most important aspect of the law that has to be explained. Therefore a practice theory of the law must illuminate how participants can be said to perform in a common world, what makes the world of law common, and how disagreements between participants about the purportedly common world are framed and adjudicated.

Patterson's paper provides a good conclusion of this volume, because it illustrates that the role of concepts in the law is not confined to the operation of the law, as emphasised in the papers that focused on concepts in their law stating function, but that concepts also play a role in our very understanding of the law's nature. Whether the contributions in this volume cover the full range of roles that concepts play in the law is a matter that remains to be seen. That they give an attractive overview of at least a number of these roles and that they point out directions for further research is clear.

An Essay on Legal Concept Formation

Åke Frändberg

1 Introduction

In view of the exceedingly important role the use of concepts of various kinds plays in law it is undoubtedly a trifle surprising that within analytical jurisprudence the question of the functions of legal concept formation in general has been subjected to so little analysis.

From one point of view, law is a technology of rules and concepts and this technology makes use of concepts with very different functions and of varying logical status. Concepts of and about law have no given meaning that is fixed for all time. They are concepts that have a function in legal argumentation, either by reason of their inclusion in the formulation of legal problems or their solutions, or because they provide the very framework for legal argumentation. In law, concepts and argumentation coalesce to form one unit. Not that the idea that legal concepts ought to be analysed on the basis of their function is a completely new one. Hohfeld's classic work on concepts of rights, for instance, was in fact even entitled *Fundamental Legal Conceptions as Applied in Judicial Reasoning*[1] and in his work Hohfeld surely kept the promise of its title.

In this article I shall make a rough classification of the various functions legal concepts can have. So it is not the concepts as such that are classified, but their functions. And it may well be the case that one and the same term has more than one function. An analysis of how different legal concepts function will at the same time be a study of the formation of legal concepts.

No attempt will be made here to demarcate exactly the multitude of legal concepts to which my classification applies. It is virtually impossible to apply such a demarcation, because practically any concept whatsoever can be a legal concept if it is expressed in a law or in some other legal material ('man', 'woman', 'nuts', 'per

Å. Frändberg (✉)
Uppsala University, Uppsala, Sweden
e-mail: Ake.Frandberg@jur.uu.se

[1] W.N. Hohfeld, *Fundamental Legal Conceptions as Applied in Judicial Reasoning and Other Legal Essays* (New Haven 1923).

J.C. Hage, D. von der Pfordten (eds.), *Concepts in Law*, Law and Philosophy Library 88,
DOI 10.1007/978-90-481-2982-9_1, © Springer Science+Business Media B.V. 2009

cent', and so on). But drawing such a line is not necessary at all as far as this study is concerned. Let us simply say that legal concepts are concepts of the kind that are usually to be found in standard glossaries for law students. It is obvious that in this connection various legal concepts may be more or less interesting from a legal point of view.

In this study I am concerned with concepts and conceptual matters, not with terms and terminology.

2 A Basic Distinction

I shall distinguish between the following two main functions of legal concepts: *the law-stating function* and *the juridical-operative function*.

Concepts with a law-stating function (law-concepts, concepts of law; in what follows *L-concepts*) are concepts that are used for stating the material legal content.

Concepts with a juridical-operative function (juridical concepts, concepts about law; in what follows *J-concepts*) are concepts that are used for the juridical handling of the legal content.

It might well be the case that a given term is ambiguous, in the sense that it names both an L-concept and a J-concept (*JL-terms*).

What lawyers handle – the very object of the work of lawyers – is *law*, i.e. a normative meaning-content structured in the form of legal rules and systems of such rules (legal systems) and appearing to us in the shape of language. L-concepts are concepts of (in) law in this sense of the word 'law'. But like all other crafts, the craft of the lawyer also demands a professional, technical vocabulary, or language, of its own. J-concepts are members of that language. In what follows L-concepts will be dealt with in Section 3, J-concepts in Section 4 and concepts expressed by JL-terms in Section 5.

3 L-Concepts

3.1 Different Kinds of L-Concepts

Within the L-concept category, four different distinctions will be made, designed to illustrate various functions of such concepts. A distinction is made between

1. genuine and non-genuine L-concepts;
2. official and dogmatic L-concepts;
3. L-concepts forming parts of rules (rule constituents) and those that systematise rules (systematising L-concepts);
4. L-concepts that are dependent on one particular legal system (system-dependent L-concepts) and those that are not (system-independent L-concepts).

3.2 Genuine and Non-genuine L-Concepts

An L-concept has a genuine or a non-genuine function, depending on whether it appears in genuine or non-genuine (spurious) legal statements in the sense indicated by the Swedish philosopher Ingemar Hedenius. This distinction, though clothed in different terms such as, for instance, 'norm-expression' and 'norm-description', has become world-wide accepted in legal philosophy.[2] Let us explain Hedenius' distinction with the help of an example. The legal statement

(*r*) Anyone who travels by car in Sweden must drive on the right-hand side of the road

can be understood in two different ways. If *r* appears in an official statute, it is natural to understand *r* as a normative statement, a decree, which the legislator has issued with the intention of directing a certain kind of human behaviour. Understood in this way *r* lacks a truth value – it is neither true nor false. Statements with this function are *genuine legal statements*. But suppose, for example, that I am in England and am asked by an Englishman who is about to undertake a motoring holiday in Sweden what the rules of the road are there, and that in reply I utter the (somewhat magisterial) statement *r*. When I make this reply it is not my intention – at least not in the first place – to steer the questioner's behaviour. My intention is merely to inform him of the content of Swedish law in this respect. And when *r* has this function, it is *a non-genuine legal statement*, and as such has a truth value (true, if uttered on, for example, December 5th, 2007, but false if uttered on December 5th, 1957). It is to be noted that *r* in my example has the same linguistic formulation irrespective of whether it is used in the genuine or in the non-genuine way, and that genuine and non-genuine legal statements are often formulated alike. But the non-genuine statement always contains, logically speaking, an explicit or understood clause 'according to valid law in *S* at *t*', where *S* is some society and *t* a point of time. Thus, in the non-genuine function, *r* is equivalent to the statement

(*r/ng*) Anyone who travels by car in Sweden must drive on the right-hand side of the road according to now [indexical] valid Swedish law

as long as this law is what is intended.

Thus, we say that concepts that are found in genuine legal statements are genuine L-concepts and that concepts found in non-genuine statements are non-genuine L-concepts. Consequently, the concepts 'delivery agreement'. 'commercial purchase' and 'delay' have a genuine function when they are found in the Sale of Goods Act, but a non-genuine function when they appear in a purely law-reproducing way in a textbook on the law relating to sale of goods.

However, the philosopher Anders Wedberg argues that it is 'highly probable' that a term which appears in a genuine legal statement (Wedberg himself uses the term

---

[2] I. Hedenius, *Om rätt och moral* ('On law and morals'; Stockholm 1941) 65f. See G.H. von Wright, *Norm and Action* (London 1963) 105.

'internal sentence' synonymously with this) does not have the same meaning as the same term when it appears in what Wedberg refers to as 'a sociological discussion'.[3]

If by this Wedberg means that a term can have one meaning when it appears in a genuine legal statement and another meaning when it appears in a non-genuine legal statement – which is probable – he has, without giving any reason, stated something that in actual fact destroys the distinction between genuine and non-genuine legal statements. But perhaps Wedberg means that sociological assertions concerning for example ownership (it is in connection with an analysis of the concept of ownership that the statement mentioned is made) are not *juridical* non-genuine legal statements (even though he calls also such statements 'sociological')[4]

As far as I understand, a term that appears in a genuine legal statement *must* in fact have exactly the same meaning there as the one it has when it appears in a corresponding non-genuine legal statement. A non-genuine legal statement is after all not an independent phenomenon but is always one that corresponds to a certain genuine legal statement. And certain claims as to adequacy must be made on such a correspondence relation, primarily to the effect that the factual content of what the non-genuine legal statement claims is valid law is identical with the factual content of the genuine legal statement – otherwise of course the non-genuine legal statement is not a correct rendering of the genuine one. But such an identity does not exist if a term has one meaning in the genuine legal statement and another meaning in the non-genuine one.

3.3 *Official and Dogmatic L-Concepts*

Official L-concepts we find in official texts – statutes, *travaux prêparatoires*, judgments etc. Examples from among the many thousands of them are 'judicial separation', 'right by marriage to joint property', 'power of attorney', 'rent', 'intent', 'forged document' and 'litigant'.

Dogmatic L-concepts are found in legal-dogmatic works. Examples of these are: 'causality', 'proximate cause', 'right *in rem*' and so on. Dogmatic L-concepts can, but need not, have equivalents among the official L-concepts. Legal dogmatists can quite well create their own concepts when they consider that the official battery of concepts is insufficient and, as we know, this happens now and then. Such concepts can later be incorporated in the law. Historically speaking there are also a number of concepts which, as products of academic law, are to be found in the law or are implicitly contained within it.

Furthermore, a term that expresses an official L-concept need not have the same meaning that it has when it expresses a dogmatic L-concept. In Swedish law, for instance, the official words 'negligence' and 'possession' seem to differ somewhat in

[3] A. Wedberg, 'Some Problems in the Logical Analysis of Legal Science' 17 *Theoria* (1951) 262–263.

[4] Wedberg, *Some Problems*, 260.

meaning from their dogmatic counterparts. That such divergences can arise between a concept that appears in the law and one that appears in legal dogmatic writings, even though both are clothed in the same terminology, comes as no surprise when the concepts in question are used by two different categories of persons – the legislator and the legal dogmatist – who are occupied with the same material, though from different starting points. The statements of legal dogmatics can be characterised as from a theoretical point of view *better versions* of official law, and the dogmatic L-concepts are components of such statements. Dogmatic statements often exceed mere law-reproducing.

All official L-concepts are genuine. Dogmatic L-concepts might be either non-genuine or genuine (for instance when they occur in an argument *de lege ferenda*).

3.4 Rule Constituents and Systematising L-Concepts

When one states law – whether this takes place in the genuine or in the non-genuine way – one makes use of two different kinds of concepts: rule constituents and systematising L-concepts. The former are concepts that are included in individual legal rules, either as components in the description of operative facts (legal facts) in the prerequisites expressed in a rule, or in the formulation of the legal consequences in the rule. Systematising L-concepts are included in the systematics of the material content of legal rules. Moreover, the systematics is also an element in the stating of law, whether it is a question of a systematisation in the law itself or one constructed by legal dogmatics. Systematising L-concepts are, for example, expressed by the names of different legal institutions ('purchase', 'gift', 'marriage', 'larceny') but also by terms in the more fundamental legal classification ('the law of third-party conflicts' (Ger. '*Sachenrecht*') – 'the law of contracts' (Ger. '*Obligationenrecht*'); 'private law' – 'public law').

As we know, the systematising L-concepts do not have only (or even primarily) a purely intellectual function (comprehensibility); their function is very much a normative, problem-solving one. Their prime function is to be used for diagnosing and qualifying problems of law.

With respect to systematising L-concepts the difference between official and dogmatic L-concepts often turns out to be very strong. The classical systematics of the law of property in legal dogmatics (the division into the law of third-party conflicts and the law of contracts and torts, and so on), is, for instance, not reflected in a more effective way in Swedish legislation on this field of the law, whose classification is constructed according to more 'down to earth' criteria.

3.5 System-Dependent and System-Independent L-Concepts

An L-concept that is dependent on one particular legal system is an L-concept that is wholly dependent, with regard to its meaning, on the content of a given legal system at a given point of time (for example, the law in force in Sweden on

January 1st, 2008). In this way the conceptual framework of rights – for example concerning the concept of ownership (property) – was determined in the analysis discussed by those taking part in the Scandinavian discussion on rights in the 1940s and 1950s.[5]

What that analysis amounts to is that, say, the meaning of the term 'ownership' is completely determined by the descriptions in legal rules of operative, or legal, facts and legal consequences which, in a given legal system at a given point of time, decide the generation and the extinction of ownership, as well as the legal effects of ownership. From this it follows that the Swedish ownership concept is not identical with the Norwegian one, and also that it is changed as soon as the legal rules on ownership are changed. This, however, is not the case when the concept of ownership is independent of a certain legal system.

When making statements on, say, British, French or Swedish law in some area, British, French or Swedish lawyers are usually not interested in assigning any meaning to the concepts under investigation other than precisely the meaning that is implied by British, French or Swedish legal rules. They treat these concepts as system-dependent L-concepts. However, sometimes our British, French or Swedish lawyers or jurists may feel a need of exchanging thoughts on legal matters between themselves on a more general level. They might want to discuss things like ownership, marriage or crime against property in a comparative perspective. Not least for comparative purposes a special kind of conceptual analysis can be useful.

What I have in mind is the special logical technique known as ideal-type definitions.[6] An *ideal-type* indicates something in its most extreme, or ideal, form, for example the ideal type of democracy, equality before the law or ownership. The ideal type is defined as an extreme form in one or more *dimensions*, that is to say, the respects in which something is for example democracy, equality before the law, or ownership. Hedenius' system-independent definition of ownership makes use of two dimensions: protection of possession and freedom of disposal.[7] The greater the degree of protection of possession and freedom of disposal a person enjoys in relation to a thing, the greater the degree of ownership he has to it, and maximum ownership in these two dimensions constitutes the definition of the ideal type ownership. As we all know, the degree of protection of possession and freedom of disposal can vary with respect to property of various kinds within a legal system as well as between different legal systems, and this state of affairs is reflected by the ideal-type definition in that *real types* can be placed somewhere along the various dimensions.

---

[5] See N.K. Sundby, 'Legal Right in Scandinavian Analyses', 13 *Natural Law Forum* (1968) 72–107.

[6] See M. Weber, *The Methodology of the Social Sciences* (E.A. Shils and H.A. Finch, translators and eds.; New York 1997) 88 and C. Hempel and P. Oppenheim, *Der Typusbegriff im Lichte der neuen Logik* (Leiden 1936).

[7] I. Hedenius 'Analysen av ägandebegreppet' ('The Analysis of the Concept of Ownership'), in: B. Belfrage and L. Stille (eds.), *Filosofi och rättsvetenskap* ('Philosophy and Legal Science'; Lund 1975).

A legal system that affords a high degree of protection of possession will therefore have its real type situated nearer to the ideal type in the protection of possession dimension than a legal system which affords a lower degree of protection. Thus, the ideal-type definition does justice to what are called differences of degree and allows comparisons to be made between different phenomena possessing the defined quality. In view of what has been said it is hardly necessary to point out that an ideal-type is not the same as an ideal in the normative sense.

The ideal-type technique is very rewarding for constructing system-independent L-concepts. In the context of comparative enquiries such concepts can be of great value: one constructs an ideal-type concept by the help of which one compares two or more different legal systems by establishing the position of their real types in the dimensions of the ideal type. The ideal-type becomes the *tertium* etc. *comparationis*.

It must be stressed that also system-independent concepts are L-concepts (concepts of the law). They refer in a more indirect way to two or more, or even all, legal systems.

4 J-Concepts

4.1 Different Kinds of J-Concepts

As was mentioned in Section 2 above, J-concepts are concepts that are used in the very juridical handling of the law (the legal content), and they differ from the L-concepts in, among others, the following respects.

(1) With the exception of the group of such concepts as may be termed 'ideological-juridical concepts', and which are dealt with below (Section 4.3), J-concepts have a more pronounced professional-juridical, or technical function.
(2) They are usually interdisciplinary in character – they are important in all, or at least, in many of the specialist juridical disciplines – and for this reason they are of special interest from the point of view of general jurisprudence.
(3) They often take the form of fundamental juridical concepts, that is, other concepts are defined by means of them. And for this reason too they are of special interest for general jurisprudence.

Within the class of J-concepts two main groups are distinguished: *technical-juridical concepts* and *ideological-juridical* (or *evaluative-juridical*) *concepts*. The former (presented under 4.2 below) are concerned with the purely intellectual handling of the law, and do not comprise any other value than that of intellectual stringency (for example 'legal source', 'legal rule', 'analogy'). The latter (presented under 4.3 below), on the other hand, contain as their most important ingredient a valuating attitude towards the juridical handling of the law (for example 'legality', 'equality before the law').

4.2 Technical-Juridical Concepts

4.2.1 Different Kinds of Technical-Juridical Concepts

Let us suppose that a system of technical-juridical concepts is to be constructed from scratch. One reasonable way of proceeding would be to form, initially, some idea of the need of such concepts. It seems to me that at least the following four types of such concepts are essential.

1. We need a set of concepts that would help us to *structure* the law in a logical and functional respect.
2. We need a set of concepts that would help us to indicate the phenomena to which the law is applicable and also to separate from each other the *areas of application* for different legal systems – concepts that indicate the 'dimensions' of the law.
3. We need a set of concepts that would help us to speak clearly and articulately about *the relations between law and action* – be it lawful or unlawful actions.
4. We need a set of concepts that would help us to describe in a precise manner *the methods of the professional-juridical handling of the law* (in the first place application of law and legislation, including both those actually practised and those merely proposed).

We now imagine that for each of these there is a corresponding family of J-concepts the members of which will meet the need in question, so that:

a. for 1. there is a corresponding set of *morphological J-concepts*
b. for 2. there is a corresponding set of *dimensional J-concepts*
c. for 3. there is a corresponding set of *praxeological J-concepts*
d. for 4. there is a corresponding set of *methodological J-concepts*.

4.2.2 Morphological J-Concepts

There is an important branch of analytical jurisprudence that could be termed *legal morphology* (the accidence, or 'grammar', of the law). This branch is concerned with the analysis of the purely formal way in which the law is structured: the form, as abstracted from the law content, of legal rules and systems of legal rules. Concepts used for that purpose we call 'morphological J-concepts'. Concepts such as 'legal rule', '(pre)requisite', 'legal consequence', 'right', 'duty', 'competence (or power-conferring) rule', 'primary' and 'secondary rule' all belong to this category.

A number of important results have been attained in the field of legal morphology. Let me give three well-known examples. In the beginning of the 20th century the American scholar W.N. Hohfeld published an analysis of the concepts of rights (jural relations) which has become a classic as one of the most elegant results of analytical jurisprudence.[8] Roughly contemporary is Merkl's and Kelsen's

[8] Hohfeld, *Fundamental Legal Conceptions*.

Stufenbau theory.[9] Here it is a question of uncovering the fundamental formal structure ('the skeleton') of more developed systems of legal rules of the type represented by national legal systems. The third example, important in all its simplicity, is the well-known distinction between the prerequisite(s) and the legal consequence of a legal rule. This means that every legal rule, either singly or in conjunction with other legal rules, can be reconstructed according to the model 'if..., then shall (may, must not) ...', where the antecedent (expressing the prerequisites) indicates certain legal, or operative, facts and the consequent indicates certain legal consequences.

By taking as a starting point the key concept 'legal rule' it is possible within legal morphology to differentiate between two different levels – one *micro-morphological* and one *macro-morphological*. At the former level it is the component parts of individual legal rules that are studied and here we meet concepts such as 'prerequisite', 'legal consequence', the various concepts of rights and duties (legal positions), the various normative modalities 'shall', 'may', 'must not', 'ought to' (obligation, permission, prohibition), and so on. Here legal morphology comes into very close contact with deontic logic. The aim of micro-morphological analysis, one could say, is to lay bare the internal structure of legal rules of various kinds. In the process an attempt can be made to reproduce rules of a certain kind to *a standard form* for rules of this type.

At the macro-morphological level the phenomena studied are the legal rules as units, incorporated in *systems* of legal rules (legal systems). Macro-morphology differentiates and examines legal rules of different kinds and also various kinds of relations that can prevail between legal rules in a legal system. In fact it is the existence of such relations that makes it possible at all for a mass of rules to be apprehended as a system. The aim of macro-morphology is ultimately to arrive at a theory concerning the construction (structure) of legal systems taken as wholes.

4.2.3 Dimensional J-Concepts

The morphological (structural) aspect of a legal rule is obviously only one aspect among many others from which law can be studied. After all, a legal rule also stands in many and complicated relations to phenomena external to it. Indeed, one important characteristic is that in certain circumstances it shall be *applied* to some factual situation belonging to a certain set of such situations. Let us call such a set *the area of operation for a legal rule*. One important aspect of the legal rule is consequently the one that concerns the relation between the legal rule and its corresponding area of operation. At a more general level it is possible to speak in a corresponding way of the area of operation for a whole legal system.

The area of operation of a legal rule is not an unambiguous, 'linear', phenomenon but is determined in at least three dimensions: a material, a spatial and a temporal dimension. The material dimension of a rule, r, demarcates the factual situations

[9] H. Kelsen, *Introduction to the Problems of Legal Theory* (transl. by B. Litschewski Paulson and S.L. Paulson; Oxford 1992) chapter V.

(states of affairs) to which r is applicable solely as regards its content (or meaning). The spatial dimension demarcates the factual situations to which r is applicable solely with regard to the geographical location of the factual situations. The temporal dimension demarcates the factual situations to which r is applicable solely with regard to when the factual situations took place. Let us say that the material dimension determines the material sphere, M, of r, the spatial dimension the spatial sphere, S, of r, and the temporal dimension the temporal sphere, T, of r. *r's* area of operation, O, can then be defined as the intersection of the sets M, S and T. A set of concepts, all of which can be described as 'dimensional', is linked with each of the three dimensions.

As to the material sphere, however, M of r is a more sophisticated set of states of affairs than the set L of r whose members are the legal facts covered by the prerequisites of r according to ordinary semantic understanding of these prerequisites (that is, if they are interpreted according to ordinary use of language). This is a consequence of what might be called 'the dilemma of the judge's application of law'. The 'dilemma' is the following. On the one hand the judge is under an obligation to decide every case of a legal character that is submitted to him (given that formal requirements such as jurisdiction are met) – the prohibition of denial of justice. On the other hand, the fact that the judge is under a duty to decide does not mean that he is free to go his own way in situations where the law is obscure or even silent. He is bound by loyalty to the existing legal system: he shall interpret the law, or create a new norm, 'in the spirit of the law'. The judge has to decide, but the law is silent. As he cannot apply some legal rule directly, he uses the legal system in an indirect, or mediate, way, thereby being, in a more remote manner, loyal to the existing law while not violating the prohibition of denial of justice. As a consequence, a statutory provision can have *a sphere of influence* exceeding its 'linguistic sphere of application' by way of extensions or analogies. But it also happens that the judge does not apply a certain statutory provision to a case which without any doubt whatsoever falls under the provision; in the juridical vocabulary, he makes a reduction of (the linguistic sphere of) the rule. This makes the family of dimensional J-concepts within the material sphere rather extensive. It includes concepts like 'linguistic sphere of application', 'sphere of influence', 'proper', 'extensive', 'analogous', 'reductive' (in extreme form leading to 'desuetude'), 'restrictive', and '*e contrario*' application of law.

As to the temporal sphere, we find dimensional concepts such as 'being in force', 'retroactivity', 'simulactivity', 'infraactivity', '*factum praeteritum*', '*factum pendens*', '*factum futurum*', 'retropendens', 'infrapendens' etc.[10]

---

[10] See my analysis of basic concepts of transitional law (i.e. concepts within the temporal sphere) in Å. Frändberg, 'Retroactivity, Simulactivity, Infraactivity' in J. Bjarup and M. Blegvad (eds.), *Time, Law and Society* (*Archiv für Rechts- und Sozialphilosophie, Beiheft 64*, 1995) 55–72. Also included in Å. Frändberg, *Rättsordningens idé. En antologi i allmän rättslära* (Uppsala 2005), 131–150.

As to the spatial sphere, basic concepts are among many others '(area of) jurisdiction', 'connection' ('case c has connections with legal system(s) $L(L', L''\ldots)$)', 'connecting factor' – all familiar concepts in private international law.

4.2.4 Praxeological J-Concepts

The relation between norm and action is close. For good reasons it could even be called a logical one, since the phenomena that are obligatory, prohibited or permitted are acts (individual or generic). I agree with Jaap Hage in that what is relevant from the point of view of norms is the so-called 'ought-to-do', not the 'ought-to-be', which latter rather can be regarded as relevant from the point of view of evaluation.[11]

Both in the administration of law and the debate about legal policy it is sometimes necessary to speak of the observance (following, complying with) and breach of legal rules. But what is meant by this? The praxeological concepts 'to observe' and 'to break a legal rule' are not unambiguous. They are logically dependent on the normative modality of the legal rule. A breach of an obligation is not the same as a breach of a prohibition and a genuine permission cannot be broken at all (it is always followed). And in order to understand, for instance, the nature of the competence norm or the statutory definition, we must have a clear idea about what it means to break such rules.

Praxeological concepts are also necessary for describing the relation between legal systems and society (social reality), which is a special case of the relation between norm and reality.[12] Let us say that legal rules are teleologically justified, if the following causal relation exists between the complying with a rule and some social state of affairs desired by the issuer of the rule:

> (TJ) If the legal consequence is realised when a legal fact (a situation described by the prerequisites of the rule) has occurred or still occurs, then the social state of affairs desired by the issuer is (probably) brought about.

That the legal consequence is realised means, with respect to obligatory rules, that certain actions are performed and, with respect to prohibitions, that certain actions are not performed.

A given legal rule can be more or less *efficient* as an instrument for achieving the desired state of affairs. For a rule to be efficient, two necessary conditions must be fulfilled:

(i) the rule must be expedient for this purpose, and
(ii) it must on the whole be observed by its addressees.

---

[11] J. Hage, 'Apropos of *A Treatise of Legal Philosophy and General Jurisprudence*: Volume 5' 20 *Ratio Juris* (2007) 439–440.

[12] On this relation see Å. Frändberg, 'The Relation between Norm and Reality as a Key to the Understanding of Law', in: W. Krawietz, R.S. Summers, O. Weinberger, G.H. von Wright (eds.), *The Reasonable as Rational? On Legal Argumentation and Justification. Festschrift for Aulis Aarnio* (Berlin 2000). Also in *Rättsordningens idé*. 97–106.

For however expedient a rule is, it is not efficient if it is not, at least on the whole, followed. Hence, in order to describe and discuss the justification of a legal rule as well as the efficiency of it we must make use of praxeological concepts.

A notorious term in legal discourse is *validity*. One reason for the great disunity within legal philosophy as to the meaning of this term is that there is disagreement already about whether it expresses a morphological, methodological, praxeological, or even an evaluative (moral) concept. There are good reasons for taking 'validity' as expressing a praxeological concept. One is that one seems to be saying something unreasonable if one says that a rule is valid even though it is in fact not applied by the courts of law or other authorities. It could be said that rule *r* is valid in society *S* at time *t*, if and only if *r* is on the whole applied by the authorities in *S* at *t* if actualised. This definition is of a praxeological character since the concept 'be applied' is a praxeological one (meaning 'be observed by the authorities'). By attaching the label 'valid' to a legal rule one indicates that the rule functions in *S* at *t*.

'Application' belongs to an important subset of praxeological terms, namely praxeological terms that are not only of a technical-juridical character (belonging to the professional language) but also give names to typical professional-juridical activities, such as 'interpretation', 'qualification', 'evaluation of evidence', 'choice of individual legal consequence (sanction)' etc.

4.2.5 Methodological J-Concepts

The methodological J-concepts can be divided into two different categories, sources of law concepts and programmatic concepts.

(1) We need a set of concepts concerning the factual basis of the legal rules, that is to say, texts, utterances, usages etc. from which according to certain more or less elaborated methods lawyers in general derive legal rules – what are called sources of law. We can call such concepts *sources of law concepts* and among them we find concepts such as 'statutory law', 'statute', 'act', 'case law', 'precedent', 'custom', 'practice', '*travaux préparatoires*' – and not least the concept 'source of law' itself.
(2) Programmatic concepts are methodological in a more genuine sense, representing, as they do, the principles guiding legal reasoning, and especially interpretative reasoning.

The doctrine of juridical method, as it is presented in textbooks on jurisprudence, can be seen as a collection of programmes indicating how lawyers in general, within the frame of their respective professional roles and the institutional forms of their activities, should proceed when they derive general legal rules from sources of law and individual legal norms from general legal rules. The names of such programmes (somewhat varying from country to country although the concepts corresponding to them are very much the same) express *programmatic concepts* and some examples are 'literal', 'linguistic', 'logical-grammatical', 'systemic', 'objective', 'subjective', 'intentional', 'teleological', 'pragmatic' and 'consequentialist interpretation'. The never-ending debate on methodological matters among jurists and lawyers would no doubt gain much from a clarification and systematisation of the concepts belonging to this family.

But also the programmes for the technique of legislative drafting belong to the doctrine of juridical method. While administration of law is endowed with a lot of accompanying programmes, the reverse is the case where the drafting of legislation is concerned. This is due to the fact that not until recently legal science – mainly in the German-speaking world – has started to develop a theory and methodology of legislation in a more comprehensive and organised way. We have long had to content ourselves with stereotyped distinctions such as 'casuistic-synthetic (generalising) law-drafting'.

4.3 Ideological-Juridical J-Concepts

However, lawyers and jurists do not only need concepts by the help of which they can handle law technically. They also examine law and its handling from an evaluative point of view – and, indeed, shall do so. It is a matter of comparing actual law and law-handling to certain standards of *good* law and law-handling. For that purpose certain instruments are needed. Such instruments consist of fruitful and precise concepts. Let us call them 'ideological-juridical concepts' as opposed to the technical-juridical ones. Among them we find concepts like 'legality', '*Rechtsstaat*' ('law-state'), 'the Rule of Law', 'legal certainty', 'legal equality', 'legal safety' and 'legal accessibility', all of which are fundamental to our legal culture.

It may appear strange to regard such concepts as 'operative-juridical', that is, as concepts used for the legal handling of the law. The reason for doing so is due to the following circumstance. In creating and applying law technique and ideology are closely interwoven. The ideal of legal certainty, for example, has undoubtedly had a profound effect on the shaping of both legislative technique and the choice of principles of statutory interpretation. The name 'ideological-juridical concepts' has been chosen simply because these concepts constitute the components of something that can be said to be the special ideology of lawyers and jurists in general in modern law-states, and this ideology deals to no small degree with the way the legal technique is to be constructed. For that reason the technical as well as the ideological concepts have been assigned to the same category, J-concepts.

The ideological-juridical concepts are, most of them at least, normative entities of the kind called 'principles'. These ideological-juridical principles are primarily not concerned with the social conditions of individuals but with the very handling of the law, and it is in this respect that they differ from other so-called legal principles such as, for instance, the general fault liability rule.

As to the logical relations between the ideological-juridical concepts it seems natural to regard '*Rechtsstaat*' – or, better, the '*Rechtsstaat*-ideology' – and 'The Rule of Law' as a kind of umbrella concepts, covering (roughly the same) legal principles, mainly legality, legal certainty, equality, safety and accessibility. Among the latter, legality occupies a place apart. That legality obtains is, as I see it, a condition for legal certainty etc. to obtain. Further distinctions can be made. With respect to legal equality for example, we can distinguish between equality in the law, before the law and through the law.[13]

The concepts mentioned designate something that societies can enjoy to a greater or less extent, and for this reason the ideological-juridical concepts are especially suitable for analysis by means of the ideal-type technique (see Section 3.5 above). The concept 'legal certainty', for example, can be regarded as a three-dimensional ideal-type concept, where a society enjoys the greater degree of legal certainty, the greater degree

(i) to which it has clear and unambiguous rules providing answers to questions of a legal kind,
(ii) to which these answers are available to all and
(iii) to which people can depend on the answers in their actions.

5 JL-Terms

As was noted in Section 2 above there is nothing to prevent a certain term from being ambiguous in the respect that it expresses both a L-concept and a J-concept. Such terms – JL-terms – have a certain capacity for bringing about confusion in legal thinking, and the reason for this will be touched upon by means of one or two examples.

The concept 'analogy' is a J-concept that plays an important role in legal thinking. The analogy can be understood as a certain type of relation between legal rules, based on a certain kind of resemblance between them (rule r as applied to case c is analogous to rule r' as applied to case c'). Now it may well happen that the legislator is interested in regulating, in some particular area of the law, the construction of rules by the courts by means of analogy. He may, for instance, wish to counteract the creation of rules detrimental to the accused by means of analogy where criminal law is concerned. If a prohibition to that effect is issued in the law the concept of analogy thereby becomes an element in a rule, that is, an L-concept.

But as soon as a concept becomes an L-concept, it starts to have a life of its own. After a while the courts perhaps discover that the analogy ban cannot be upheld to the letter. Hence they begin redefining the concept 'analogy' by stating that certain analogies are not analogies at all but 'extensions' that are not covered by the ban. Such redefinitions can be explained by the teleological justification of the rule in question and can be completely justified when the analogy concept is an L-concept.

On the other hand, it would lead to absurd consequences if this analogy concept were to be used in general discussions about analogies or in presentations of the

[13] See Å. Frändberg, 'Legal Equality', in P. Wahlgren (ed.), *Perspectives on Jurisprudence. Essays in Honor of Jes Bjarup* (Scandinavian Studies in Law 48; Stockholm 2005).

concept in textbooks on jurisprudence, that is, if the analogy concept as a J-concept were to be identified with the analogy concept as an L-concept. The circumstances that influence the forming of the L-concept are special for the particular area of law to which it belongs and circumstances relevant there are often of no interest at all when a technical J-concept with the same name is defined. Such a concept must be defined on purely intellectual grounds and one must be on one's guard against (crypto) normative influences when defining the concept.

'Retroactivity' is another example of a JL-term. Also here is the case that interpretation in legal practice of a legislative ban on retroactivity can assign to the retroactivity concept, as an L-concept, a content that is quite impossible as a content of a general retroactivity concept of the J-type.

A certain vigilance is therefore justified when dealing with terms that have a dual function of this kind.

6 Conclusion

In this essay I have tried to contribute to the part of analytical jurisprudence, or legal philosophy, that investigates legal concept formation. In doing so, I have consciously adopted a very abstract approach in that the concepts examined have in a way been taken out of their contexts. In reality, of course, the concepts do not function in isolation but as components of legal argumentation, and their meaning must always be determined according to their function in such argumentation.

However, and this must be emphasised, the question here has not been that of clarifying individual concepts – this would necessarily involve a contextual approach – but rather of systematising the contexts themselves. Some contexts state the law, others are of a morphological kind, others again are methodological and so on, and my view is that when a clarification of an individual concept is made, the family to which it belongs should be taken into account. So the abstract approach in this essay does not conflict at all with the idea of a contextual explication; on the contrary it should be seen as a step in that direction.

Moreover, the two activities of concept formation and theory formation are in practice indissolubly bound to another. As Carl G. Hempel has pointed out, 'concept formation and theory formation in science ... (are) so closely interrelated as to constitute virtually two different aspects of the same procedure'.[14] This is not least apparent in legal science. The construction of, say, a morphological or a methodological theory within jurisprudence or legal philosophy is therefore very much a concept forming activity. Likewise there is a close similarity verging on coalescence between concept formation and law formation. In Western legislation as well as in Western science, the central role of concept formation is connected with the fact that, viewed historically, these two activities rest on a common ideological base – the

[14] C.G. Hempel, *Fundamentals of Concept Formation in Empirical Science* (Chicago 1952) 1–2.

rationalism that to such a high degree has informed European culture since Greek and Roman antiquity.

In this essay I have collected a huge amount of legal concepts, of as well as about law, all of them fruitful objects for philosophical analysis. The day legal philosophy wakes up and realises that there are other concepts than the concept of law itself to be examined, it will find a rich field for investigation in legal thinking itself, the study of which can illuminate the phenomena of law and legal science in a far more rewarding way than, for example, the endless, somewhat sterile discussions about positivism (exclusive and inclusive) and natural law theories – topics a world apart from central ideas in legal thinking. A cause for this unfortunate development within legal philosophy in recent decades is, I think, that legal philosophy has almost totally been swallowed up by moral philosophy. As a consequence, we do not, I am sorry to say, learn very much about legal thinking from most of contemporary legal philosophy.

About Concepts in Law

Dietmar von der Pfordten

1 Introduction

In its mainstream, modern legal theory is characterised by two fundamental reductionisms. First: Law isn't understood any more with reference to necessary aims like justice (Plato, Aristotle, Radbruch), self-preservation (Hobbes), property (Locke), or freedom (Kant, Hegel), but only to contingent means. One might call this 'instrumentalism'. Second: The plurality of the decisive means and elements of law is – with notable exceptions[1] – silently and implicitly reduced to norms, rules and/or principles, and neglects (or at least downsizes) alternatives like concepts, institutes or institutions. One might call this 'normativism'.[2] For example Kelsen's 'Pure Theory of Law' ('Reine Rechtslehre') does not any more assume a necessary aim of the law and it does not any more consider concepts, institutes or institutions as decisive parts of the law. And the same is true for H. L. A. Hart's 'The Concept of Law'. Together the means-model and the norms/rules/principles-model of law dominate everything.

First of all, it is crucial to understand that both reductionisms are not independent of each other but hang together – not logically, but justificatorily: If necessary aims of law are considered to play a decisive role, the means to attain these aims of law can be, to quite a great extent, contingent, pluralistic and variable. If necessary aims of law are thought to play no role at all, instead being only arbitrary means, the means as factual features of law become decisive to attain these arbitrary aims and to distinguish law from other social facts like morals, conventions, and political power. In this case, the means tend to develop a monistic hegemony. We face the

D. von der Pfordten (✉)
University of Göttingen, Göttingen, Germany
e-mail: dpfordt@gwdg.de

[1] Robert Summers, *Form and Function in a Legal System* (Cambridge 2006); Neil MacCormick, *Institutions of Law. An Essay in Legal Theory* (Oxford 2007).
[2] For example Manuel Atienza and Juan Ruiz Manero, *A Theory of Legal Sentences* (Dordrecht 1998), XI: 'Legal sentences are, in our view, the most elementary units of law.'

J.C. Hage, D. von der Pfordten (eds.), *Concepts in Law*, Law and Philosophy Library 88,
DOI 10.1007/978-90-481-2982-9_2, © Springer Science+Business Media B.V. 2009

norms/rules/principles-model as the main expression of this monistic hegemony of the means in modern legal theory.

The overall aim of this article is to attack normativism.[3] This attack on normativism will be launched via the more limited thesis that concepts play a major role in law, an even greater role than norms. It will be argued that conceptual analysis is important in law, in many cases even more important than the analysis of norms. So in this article only one aspect of the second reductionism will be discussed extensively: the neglect (or, at the least, the downsizing) of concepts in modern legal theory.[4]

2 The Importance of Concepts

Nobody can deny that modern law is comprised of norms or rules or principles. But not only in normal but especially in hard cases, concepts like human dignity, life, liberty, art, science, religion, property, contract, fraud, negligence, and murder, as well as their interpretation, play a decisive role. The norms or rules or principles in which these concepts occur are often only the outer costume, that is, the outer means to cause the recipient to fulfil the required action. But the main question of content and of adjudication is frequently one of conceptual analysis.

Take for example the concept 'art' in article 5 Section 3 of the German Constitution: 'Art and science are free'. In this article 5 Section 3 a fundamental right to freedom of art is stated. This normative statement is similar to the statement of other fundamental rights in the constitution. Like for other human rights, e.g. the freedom of belief in art. 4, there is a specific form in the technicality of the limitation of this fundamental right of art, which depends on the specific form of the normative statement (in this case without legal proviso). But the crucial question for the application of this norm and therefore the protection of this fundamental right is: What is art? Or more specifically: What is an artistic action in comparison to e.g. an action of business, politics, or religion? This question can only be answered by a conceptual analysis of the concept 'art'. Consequently, the German Bundesverfassungsgericht discussed different interpretations of the concept 'art'.[5] It refused to come to its own definitive conclusion about the concept. But this opinion only transferred the decision from the court to society in general.

There seems to be a great variety of concepts in the law. This variety ranges from descriptive concepts (road), over evaluative concepts (good manners), to norma-

---

[3] For a first attempt to attack normativism, see: Dietmar von der Pfordten, 'Zum Verhältnis von Begriffen, insbesondere im Recht', in: Bernd Schünemann, Marie-Theres Tinnefeld, Roland Wittmann (eds.), *Gerechtigkeitswissenschaft – Kolloquium aus Anlass des 70. Geburtstages von Lothar Philipps* (Berlin 2005), 205–224.

[4] For an attack on instrumentalism, see: Dietmar von der Pfordten, 'What is Law? Aims and Means', forthcoming.

[5] Decisions of the Bundesverfassungsgericht: BVerfGE 30, 173, 189; 67, 213, 226ff.; 75, 369, 377; 83, 130, 138; judgment of the first senate: 13/6/2007 – 1 BvR 1783/05.

tive concepts (obligation). It ranges from natural or cultural but non-technical and, therefore, initially non-juristic, day-to-day concepts like human being, life, art, profession, science, religion, action, company, animal, vertebrate, norm etc. on the one hand, to quite technical, inner-systematic concepts created totally or nearly totally by the rules of the factual legal system like surety, mortgage and standing in a trial, on the other hand. In between these two extremes of non-technical day-to-day concepts and technical law-created concepts, we find concepts which have a non-legal background but some minor or major legal shaping, like ownership, possession, person, claim, judgment, contract, offer, and will. I call this continuum of legal influence the 'continuum of legal-systematic determination of non-legal concepts.'

Legal systems seem to implement themselves into our general understanding of the world as well by taking up natural, cultural and mainly descriptive day-to-day-concepts like action, human being, and life, these being relatively unchanged as by shaping other originally natural or cultural concepts like ownership, claim, possession, person. In what follows, an attempt will be made to elucidate the decisive role of concepts in the law and the importance of conceptual analysis in five steps. First, it will be asked what concepts are, as this is, at the most fundamental level, crucial to the attack on normativism. Second, the appropriate method for conceptual analysis will be scrutinised. Third, it will be questioned how concepts are related to each other in a conceptual scheme in general. Fourth, this understanding of a conceptual scheme in general will be transferred to the conceptual scheme of the law. Fifth, in a sort of conclusion, it will be questioned as to whether concepts or norms are more decisive for legal reasoning.

3 What Are Concepts?

Normativism is based on a very fundamental understanding – or (in my opinion) better said: misunderstanding of concepts. So in order to attack normativism it is necessary to inquire into the nature of concepts.

There are four classical alternatives in the history of ideas to determine what concepts are:

(1) idealism: concepts or forms are non-representational entities independent of other non-conceptual natural or social entities (Plato), e.g. independent of natural subjects or substances[6];
(2) realism: concepts are non-representational properties of other singular natural or social entities. Therefore, they are the reference (Bedeutung) of predicates/ concept-words (Begriffsworte) in subject-predicate sentences (Frege, Carnap)[7]

[6] Plato, *Euthyphro* 5d3, 6b9-13, *Politeia* 505aff.

[7] Gottlob Frege, *Die Grundlagen der Arithmetik* (Stuttgart 1987), 15f.; Gottlob Frege, 'Über Begriff und Gegenstand', in G. Frege, *Funktion, Begriff, Bedeutung* (6th edition G. Patzig Goettingen 1986), 67f., 72; Rudolf Carnap, *Logical Foundations of Probability* (2nd edition Chicago 1962), 7f.

or – in another version – the sense (Sinn) of these predicates/ concept-words (Begriffsworte) (Peacocke)[8];

(3) conceptualism: concepts are mental representations in individual humans and perhaps higher animals of internal or external properties or entities (Ockham, Descartes, Locke, Leibniz, Hume, Kant, Fodor, Margolis/Laurence, Prinz)[9] (which does not mean that they are pictures of those properties or entities);

(4) nominalism: concepts are representational units of language, that is, words or connections of words or similar parts of linguistic systems of representation (Hobbes, Wittgenstein, Quine, Jackson, many modern philosophers of language).[10]

Here I can only sketch a few reasons for a decision:

(a) Idealism is metaphysically obscure and queer. But even if such metaphysically obscure and queer entities like platonic ideas or forms existed, they would have to be perceived in some way. So we would still need some sort of mental representation of them. Idealism and conceptualism, therefore, do not contradict each other. It is simply necessary to use different terms to refer to them. As so many deny the existence of these superhuman entities like platonic ideas or forms but accept the talk about concepts as meaningful, it makes no sense to reserve the expression and concept 'concept' for these superhuman entities. So they should be named otherwise, e.g. 'platonic ideas or forms'. These platonic ideas are not the subject of this article. To discuss them would be a totally different metaphysical endeavour.

(b) Realism is possible as an ontological theory. But there seems to be no reason to reduce concepts to properties, or, at the least, blur the distinction between properties as parts of facts and concepts of properties as mental representations of these properties as parts of facts. For example, we carefully distinguish between 'law' and the 'concept of law.' If somebody knows the concept of law – like it is presented in H. L. A. Hart's famous book –, he does not know law. He does not know all the singular instantiations of law and therefore law in its entirety as a social fact or as a property of modern society, e.g. English, French, Italian

---

[8] Christopher Peacocke, *A Study of Concepts* (Cambridge 1992), 3.

[9] Wilhelm Ockham, *Summa Logicae* (2nd edition Hamburg 1999); Rene Descartes, *Meditationes de prima philosophiae*, part. III, sec. 5 ff.; *Principia Philosophiae*, part I, sec. 13ff.; John Locke, *An Essay Concerning Human Understanding* (New York 1959), introd., 32; book II, 1, 1; Immanuel Kant, *Kritik der reinen Vernunft*, (2nd edition, Akademieausgabe Vol. III), 85; Jerry Fodor, *Concepts. Where Cognitive Science Went Wrong* (Oxford 1998); Eric Margolis and Stephen Laurence, 'Concepts and Cognitive Science', in Eric Margolis and Stephen Laurence (eds.), *Concepts. Core Readings* (Cambridge 1999) 7; Jesse J. Prinz, *Furnishing the Mind. Concepts and their Perceptual Basis* (Cambridge 2004) 1, 3, passim.

[10] Thomas Hobbes, *De Corpore*, 1. part, Ch. 2, Sec. 9; Ludwig Wittgenstein, *Philosophische Untersuchungen, Werkausgabe Bd. 1* (Frankfurt a. M. 1984) §§ 96, 383; Willard V. O. Quine, *Word and Object* (Cambridge 1960), 3, 12, 161, 270f.; Frank Jackson, *From Metaphysics to Ethics. A Defence of Conceptual Analysis* (Oxford 2000), 30, 33.

and German Private, Criminal, Administrative and Constitutional Law, and so on. He only knows some very general qualifications of law.

(c) Conceptualism is e.g. validated by the assumption that we understand concepts, e.g. by the synonymy or near synonymy of propositions like these two: 'Peter has acquired the concept of law.' and 'Peter has understood what law is.'

But concepts as mental representations are only one element of our thinking and understanding. So in order to understand conceptualism we face the crucial question concerning our thinking and our understanding of the world: Which part of our thinking is more decisive: concepts or judgments?[11] Both concepts and judgments are tools to understand the world. But we have to realise that their contribution differs because they differ from each other. Understanding the world presupposes singular sensations, like a singular colour sensation or a singular sound sensation. In order to understand the complexity of our world, these singular sensations must be combined. There are two possibilities to fulfil this task: I call this the singular-solution and the concept-solution. The singular-solution might connect every singular sensation in its singularity, so that one gets an unlimited combination of singular sensations of the form $X_1 - X_N$. The conceptual-solution does not individualise all sensations over all their different qualities, but only concerning their situation in time and space, while all other qualities are combined by several properties which are – as faculties of our minds – concepts. Both solutions are logically possible. But factually, the singular-solution, which is the necessary complement of nominalism, is impossible in a world of limited memory. We are able to grasp an unlimited amount of sensory data, but we are not able to store it. Additionally, the singular-solution is unfavourable because of ontological and linguistic reasons. If things which are considered to be stable in time and space were only recognizable by singular sensations, it would be impossible for us to become accustomed to this stability and distinguish the knowledge of these stable things from momentous impressions like reflections in the air or singular sounds. It would also be impossible to refer to our unlimited sensations with a limited quantity of words. So the singular-solution is epistemologically impossible in a world of limited mental resources and ontologically and linguistically very unsatisfactory. Therefore, there is no reason to be sceptical about our common-sense view which is in accordance with the view of cognitive science and psychology that we use concepts to acquire sensual knowledge. To fulfil their purpose, there are no further qualifications of concepts necessary. For example it is not necessary to understand concepts as pictures of reality.

With the acknowledgement of concepts in our process of perception, it has, as of yet, not been shown that concepts are decisive in comparison to judgments or thoughts. The reason to argue for this is as follows: If concepts are the tool to combine singular sensations, then they are nearer to these sensations than judgments or thoughts. Judgments or thoughts do not combine sensations

[11] A third possibility would certainly be that they are equally or roughly equally decisive.

directly; they do this only indirectly, by combining concepts. So if sensations are the basis of our knowledge of the world, concepts are nearer than judgments or thoughts to this basis of our knowledge. Therefore, they are generally more decisive than judgments or thoughts.

This also holds in comparison to normative thoughts or judgments. Normative thoughts (or norms understood as thoughts) are a special group of thoughts. Normative thoughts, in addition to descriptive thoughts, include the will of the speaker that a certain action shall be performed or a certain condition attained. But this additional function is based upon the epistemological function of the concepts which are part of the norm. Like concepts in judgments, these concepts are nearer to our sensations as fundaments of our perception of the world. So concepts are more fundamental in respect of their fundament in the factual world than normative thoughts, that is, norms (understood as thoughts).[12]

Additionally, concepts can have not only an epistemological function, but also an evaluative (and, therefore, justificatory) function. If an action is qualified by the concept good, this justifies its performance.

The rejection of the dominance of thoughts over concepts on the level of understanding/thinking doesn't exclude the assumption of the so-called context-principle on the level of language, that is, the assumption that the meaning of propositions/sentences determines the meaning of words.

(d) Nominalism is a form of reductionism of concepts as mental representations to linguistic entities like words and connections of words. There is a close historical and justificatory link between the reductionism of nominalism which is accepted by many modern philosophers, e.g. Hobbes, Wittgenstein, Quine, Jackson and many philosophers of language, and the two fundamental reductionisms of modern legal theory, that is, instrumentalism and normativism, mentioned in the introduction. This link can only be sketched briefly here:

First: If concepts are only words or connections of words then they are contingent like words are. They are arbitrarily invented and abandoned like different words in different languages are invented and abandoned arbitrarily for different arbitrary means. So concepts like justice, self-preservation, property or freedom cannot be necessary in their content. Therefore, they cannot deliver a necessary content to build up necessary aims. As a consequence, the law cannot have necessary aims. So instrumentalism is justified.

[12] See for this classical view: Emil Lask, 'Rechtsphilosophie', in: Emil Lask, *Gesammelte Schriften I,* (Tübingen 1923) 315f.; Philipp Heck, *Begriffsbildung und Interessenjurisprudenz* (Tübingen 1932) 9, 38, 52f.; Gustav Radbruch, *Rechtsphilosophie* (Studienausgabe 2nd edition Heidelberg 2003), 106–118; Karl Larenz, *Methodenlehre der Rechtswissenschaft* (6th edition Berlin 1991), 437f. The dismissal of the so-called 'conceptual jurisprudence' ('Begriffsjurisprudenz') by Heck, Larenz and others did not deny that concepts are a decisive part of the law. Only the deductive inference of new concepts from existing concepts in the application of the law is criticised. Heck states this explicitly on p. 9.

Second: If concepts are only words or connections of words then they can only be relevant to fulfil their function as tools of representation as parts of sentences, that is, propositions understood as units of language. Then Frege's context-principle applies[13]: Only in the context of a sentence/proposition do words, that is, in the view of nominalism, concepts, have meaning. This holds also for normative sentences/propositions, that is, norms (understood as speech acts). Therefore, it is sufficient to analyse norms (understood as speech acts). So normativism would be justified.

Thus, the crucial question for an attack on normativism is: Is nominalism convincing? At least four arguments count against the nominalistic reduction of concepts to linguistic entities:

(1) Different words in different languages like 'tree', 'arbre' and 'Baum' are connected in our understanding with one concept. If somebody knows what a tree is and knows the English term 'tree' and then learns the French translation 'arbre', he does not – in his own understanding and the understanding of others – learn a new concept, but instead only a new word in a foreign language for the same concept of a tree.

(2) Conceptualism is able to explain the widely-accepted distinction between extension ('Bedeutung' in Frege's words) and intension ('Sinn' in Frege's words) of linguistic expressions, which nominalism has difficulty in explaining. Concepts, then, are intensions of predicates, or, more precisely – but contrary to Peacocke's assumption, which was mentioned above – mental representations as intensions of predicates as meta-representations of both concepts and properties.

(3) Concepts show – as Jerry Fodor has indicated – the feature of compositionality.[14] Thoughts are determined by their constituents, that is, their concepts and other elements like logical junctions. Concepts are productive and systematic. Productivity means: There are infinitely many concepts that a person can entertain. But people's mental capacities are finite. This infinity of concepts must be representable. This condition is only met if all concepts are individuated by their syntax and their contents, and the syntax and content of complex concepts is finitely reducible to that of the primitive constituents. Systematicity means: The mind can perform certain systematic functions with concepts. For example somebody who can grasp that Mary loves John can also grasp that John loves Mary.

(4) We can explain the difference between thinking (and, therefore, concepts as parts of thoughts) and speaking (and, therefore, words as parts of sentences) with respect to different functions. Language first has the function to enable us to communicate with each other, and second, to sustain our memory. Thinking

---

[13] Gottlob Frege, *Die Grundlagen der Arithmetik* (Stuttgart 1987), 92, 94.

[14] Jerry Fodor, *Concepts. Where Cognitive Science Went Wrong* (Oxford 1998), 94f.

(and, therefore, concepts) is a primary tool to understand the world and build up a complex order of mental representations of the world. At least in a more elaborated form, this understanding is dependent on language, but this does not mean that it is identical or reducible to language. In the high days of scientific positivism, a reference to mental phenomena like concepts was dismissed as meaningless, or at least obscure. But even in analytic philosophy, the area of philosophy of mind which includes numerous references to mental phenomena is now a respectable branch. Positivism in legal theory still is based on scientific positivism to a large extent and has unfortunately not yet realised the realistic roll-back in general philosophy.

If conceptualism is accepted, concepts are not to be understood as independent things or facts. It is sufficient to assume mental processes of differentiating qualities as conceptual. Concepts are only reifications of these mental processes. In the same way that joy is a reification of being happy, a concept is a reification of understanding a property. This means 'no concept without understanding'.

4 Conceptual Analysis

The second crucial question with respect to the status of concepts is that of conceptual analysis. To answer this question, two models are dominant: a classical model and a reductionist-positivist model. The classical model of conceptual definition is an outcome of the classical doctrine that concepts are epistemologically dominant in comparison to linguistic phenomena like words and sentences.[15] The reductionist positivist model of conceptual explication is a natural and historical, although not necessary, outcome of either the realist or the nominalist view that concepts are qualities or linguistic entities like words or connections of words.

a) The classical model comprises three basic forms of definition in a wider sense:

   (1) the definition by the next higher, that is, more abstract, concept and the specific difference (definitio per genus proximum et differentiam specificam)[16] and
   (2) the determination by all the lower, that is, more concrete concepts (determinatio)
   (3) the determination by listing the real parts of the object the concept refers to (determinatio ex partibus)
   (4) one could add a fourth distinction between descriptive and normative elements of concepts which was emphasised for practical language by Charles L. Stevenson.[17]

---

[15] Aristotle, *Peri Hermeneias* 16a1.

[16] Aristotle, *Metaphysics* Z 12, 1037bf.

[17] Charles L. Stevenson, *Ethics and Language* (New Haven 1944).

For example, the concept ‘apple’ can then be analysed as:

(1) a fruit which is round and grows on specific trees which have the qualities a, b, c, . . .
(2) either a Boskop or Golden Delicious or Elstar or Braeburn etc.
(3) including skin, flesh, stem and kernels.
(4) a descriptive concept

Not all of these alternatives are always possible. It is e.g. impossible to determine concepts which refer to objects which are not in time and/or space by temporal or spatial parts. But even if an object is in time and/or space, a definition by its parts would be senseless if it is an artefact which can only be understood by its purpose. So, for example, a chair has no necessary temporal or spatial parts, because its only necessary (and, thus, for a definition, decisive) quality is that it is a human artefact made for one person to sit on. The same holds for many legal concepts e.g. the concept ‘weapon’. Weapons can be the most different objects, and, consequently, a definition with only a reference to necessary parts is impossible.

Is this classical model obsolete? Some think so. Already Leibniz had criticised that it seems to be impossible to distinguish between the genus proximum and the differentia specifica.[18] But this dismissal is too quick, because one could drop these ontological assumptions and just talk of necessary conditions which can add up to a necessary and sufficient combination of conditions.

A very influential part of the attack on the classical model was the famous critique of Wittgenstein in his ‘Philosophical Investigations’ and his proposal of family resemblance. But one has to read this critique very carefully; therefore, although it is well known, I will quote it here again[19]:

> 65. . . . And this is true. Instead of producing something common to all that we call language, I am saying that these phenomena have no one thing in common which makes us use the same word for all, – but that they are *related* to one another in many different ways. And it is because of this relationship, or these relationships, that we call them all “language”. I will try to explain this.
>
> 66. Consider for example the proceedings that we call “games”. I mean board-games, card-games, ball-games, Olympic games, and so on. What is common to them all? – Don’t say: “There must be something common, or they would not be called ‘games’ ” - but *look* and *see* whether there is anything common to all. – For if you look at them you will not see something that is common to *all*, but similarities, relationships, and a whole series of them at that. To repeat: don’t think, but look! – Look for example at board-games, with their multifarious relationships. Now pass to card-games; here you find many correspondences with the first group, but many common features drop out, and others appear. . . .

---

[18] Gottfried Wilhelm Leibniz, ‘Über die universale Synthese und Analyse oder über die Kunst des Auffindens und Beurteilens’, in Gottfried Wilhelm Leibniz, *Schriften zur Logik und zur philosophischen Grundlegung von Mathematik und Naturwissenschaft* (Frankfurt a. M. 1996), 135.
[19] Ludwig Wittgenstein, *Philosophische Untersuchungen, Werkausgabe Bd. 1* (Frankfurt a. M. 1984), § 65–67. Translation by G.E.M. Anscombe (*Philosophical Investigations*; Oxford 1978).

> And the result of this examination is: we see a complicated network of similarities overlapping and criss-crossing: sometimes overall similarities, sometimes similarities of detail.
>
> 67. I can think of no better expression to characterize these similarities than "family resemblances"; for the various resemblances between members of a family: build, features, colour of eyes, gait, temperament, etc. overlap and criss-cross in the same way. – And I shall say: "games" form a family.

§§ 65 and 67 seem to say that the instances of one concept like 'language' or 'game' do not have one property in common. But one has to distinguish the weaker from the stronger version to interpret Wittgenstein's thesis. The stronger version asserts that there are concepts like language or games which do not even have necessary conditions. The weaker version asserts that these concepts have some necessary conditions in common, but there is no combination of these necessary conditions forming a necessary and sufficient condition (and, therefore, a definition). Most interpreters have sided with the weaker version,[20] as it seems to be the only appropriate one, as Wittgenstein's own example of games shows: If one looks closely at the beginning of § 66 one sees that Wittgenstein characterised games as being all 'proceedings' ('Vorgänge').

'Necessary condition' does not have to mean 'a priori', or absolutely necessary. It can also mean 'relatively stable or invariant' in comparison to other, more changeable concepts of our conceptual scheme.

So the arguments of Wittgenstein provide us with no obstacle to assuming that there are necessary conditions of concepts in this weaker relative sense. The number of these necessary conditions is not limited a priori. If there are several necessary conditions, it is not logically impossible – although not necessary or provable – that together they build up a necessary and sufficient condition (and, thereby, a definition). There is – this has to be accepted – no necessity or proof that several necessary conditions add up to such a necessary and sufficient condition. We could not even determine with absolute certainty when this point has been reached. But for the practical function of concepts as tools to understand the world and to build up an order of representations, we need a relatively clear distinction between different concepts. Therefore, we assume some approximation to the ideal of necessary and sufficient condition. So, at least for most concepts, we assume that, at least approximately, necessary and sufficient conditions to distinguish the concepts from other concepts can be named – at least by some experts in the field.

b) A positivist (and, in its requirements, much reduced) model of conceptual analysis was proposed by Rudolf Carnap in his book 'Logical Foundations of Probability'[21]: It includes four criteria for 'conceptual explication':

---

[20] For this interpretation see Hjalmar Wennerberg, 'The Concept of Family Resemblance in Wittgenstein's later Philosophy' 33 *Theoria* (1967), 110; Eike von Savigny, *Wittgensteins 'Philosophische Untersuchungen'. Ein Kommentar für Leser, Bd. 1* (Frankfurt a. M. 1988), § 66, 3.

[21] Carnap, *Logical Foundations of Probability*, 7.

similarity: In most cases the explicans should be able to replace the explicandum;
exactness: The rules for the use of the explicans have to be given in an exact manner so that it can be integrated in a well-grounded system of scientific concepts;
fruitfulness: The explicans must be allowed to form as many general statements as possible;
simplicity: The explicans should be as simple as possible.

A closer look at both models shows that they are not in contradiction to each other. The classical view is a way to arrive at the first demand of Carnap's view, the demand to reach similarity. The only difference is that the classical view has, in its first part, the higher aim to give a synonymous definition which is considered questionable nowadays. Therefore, I think the two views can be combined. First, one should use the classical model in its reduced form, as mentioned above. This will – if we cannot attain a definition – provide the best way to reach similarity as the first element of Carnap's view. Then the requirements 2–4 of Carnap's view can be applied additionally.

5 How Are Concepts Related to Each Other?

The third main question concerning the status of concepts is: How are concepts related to each other? Or, more precisely, because the decisive element for the relation between concepts is the content: How are the contents of concepts connected to each other? There seem to be two main features of concepts which are decisive to answer this question: the extent, abstractness or inclusiveness of the concept and its necessity. Firstly: Concepts are, in their relation, clearly more or less abstract or inclusive, that is, their extension differs: e.g. all humans are living beings, but not all living beings are humans. And secondly: There are relations of (relative) necessity and contingency between each other. It is necessary of a human to be a living being. But it is not necessary for a living being to be a human. What can be the reason that a concept is necessary for others but not vice versa? I think there are two main reasons for necessity in the hierarchy of concepts: One reason concerns the function of very abstract concepts to systematise the whole system of concepts that is an internal function of the conceptual scheme. These are logical and ontological concepts like relation, substance, object, quality, identity, unity, necessity, possibility, consistence, coherence, etc. Kant's characterization of ideas as 'regulative' (that is, unifying) is an expression of this function.[22]

The other reason is the immediate, or nearly immediate, connection to empirical sensations, that is, an external function to represent the objects with their qualities of these sensations. Those concepts which are nearest to empirical sensations are relatively necessary, e.g. concepts like blue, loud, heavy, tree, apple, banana, tomato,

[22] Immanuel Kant, *Kritik der reinen Vernunft,* (2nd edition, Akademieausgabe Vol. III), 353f.

bird. So we have two levels of strict (or, at least, stricter) necessity in the hierarchy of concepts: a first and highest level of systematic closure of the whole conceptual scheme, and a third and medium level of highest empirical reference and influence.[23] In between these two levels of stricter necessity, we have a second level of rather high (but not highest) abstractness. On this level, conceptualisation is less, or even much less, necessary. Take for example concepts like 'fruit' or 'vegetable'. It is clear that the concepts of fruit and vegetable have a greater extension than the concepts apple, banana or tomato, and a smaller extension than the concepts quality, object or relation. But in comparison to apple, banana and peach on the one hand and thing and property on the other hand, the dividing line between fruits and vegetables is quite vague and arbitrary. Why, for example, is a tomato a vegetable, but not a fruit? So we have a level of rather abstract concepts which are quite arbitrary and vague, because they are not so clearly systematically necessary or empirically determined. On this level, we also find many theoretical concepts like 'atom', 'evolution' or 'system' which require a theory to their explanation. These theoretical concepts cannot be situated on the first level, because every theory already presupposes some most abstract concepts like relation, thing, quality, identity or difference.

There is also a fourth very low and concrete level situated below the empirical determined third level. On this level, we find e.g. the division of the concept of apples into different sorts, like Golden Delicious, Elstar, Boskop, Braeburn etc. The concepts on this level are again quite arbitrary and vague.

To sum up: We can distinguish four levels of abstraction with variations in necessity:

- a first highly abstract level with strict necessity, e.g. including concepts like object, thing, quality, identity, difference, relation, unity, substance, implication, necessity, possibility, conjunction, disjunction, consistence, coherence;
- a second rather high level of abstraction with much contingency, e.g. including concepts like fruit, vegetable, living being, human being, person, action, will, intention, freedom, atom, evolution, system, ownership;
- a medium level of abstraction with stricter empirical necessity, e.g. including concepts like apple, banana, tomato, tree, dog, cat, bird, blue, red, loud, heavy, dry;
- a low level of abstraction with much contingency, e.g. including concepts like Golden Delicious, Boskop, Elster, Braeburn.

There are no clear thresholds between these four levels. Therefore, the term 'level' would be misunderstood if it would be understood as 'step', or distinct 'category'. The levels are only different parts of the continuum of abstraction with more or less continuing differences. So, to a certain degree, the concepts on the second

[23] These concepts are identified by the prototype theory as basic concepts or prototypes. See Eleanor Rosch, 'Principles of Categorization', in: Margolis and Laurence, *Concepts. Core Readings*, 189–206; Margolis and Laurence, *Concepts and Cognitive Science*.

and first level are also influenced by the relation to empirical sensation. Additionally, the concepts on the second and third level have some function of systematisation.

There is much debate in cognitive science and philosophy of mind about the interpretation of conceptualisation; especially to explain the concepts on the third level, we have a so-called prototype-theory, a stereotype-theory and other proposals.[24] There is no space here to go into the details of this discussion, but the results we have reached so far shall be transferred to the interpretation of legal concepts.

6 Concepts in Law[25]

In a legal system both phenomena mentioned in the second and the fifth section are combined: the continuum of legal-systematic determination of non-legal concepts and the hierarchy of four levels of abstraction with variations in necessity. The first feature of the conceptual scheme of a legal system is that these concepts of a legal system also form a hierarchy of four levels of abstraction with a first inner-systematic level and a third empiricist level.[26] But there are some peculiarities in comparison to the general conceptual scheme of four levels of abstraction.

A second feature is this: Concepts of the first level of abstraction of the general conceptual scheme (like identity, difference, object or consistency) are only very seldom explicitly taken up and made part of the law by the legal conceptual system. They are used in interpreting the legal system and in adjudication, but normally they function as a sort of logical and ontological background for any legal system.

Therefore, the most abstract concepts of the legal system do not reach the abstractness of the most abstract concepts of the general conceptual system. But they fulfil the same function of systematisation. Such concepts are: obligation, permission, lawful, unlawful, right, norm, power, immunity, privilege, ownership, human being, person, human dignity, life, liberty, action, punishment.[27] Important is the fact that these concepts are mostly taken from the second level of abstraction of the general conceptual scheme, that is, the level where the content of concepts is quite contingent. This opens up the possibility for the legal system to modify these concepts and shape them according to its own purposes and values to a great extent.

---

[24] Margolis and Laurence, *Concepts and Cognitive Science*; Prinz, *Furnishing the Mind.*

[25] I do not distinguish between 'concepts in law', 'legal concepts' and 'concepts of a legal system' because I don't see good reasons for any discrimination.

[26] Ronald Dworkin, *Justice in Robes* (Cambridge 2006), 9f., 145f. distinguishes between *criterial* concepts like bachelor, *natural kind* concepts like tiger and *interpretive* concepts like justice. He maintains that the central concepts of political and personal morality – the concepts of justice, liberty, equality, democracy, right, wrong, cruelty, and insensitivity – function for us as interpretive concepts. But he leaves open the question whether all legal concepts are thus interpretive.

[27] See Wesley Newcomb Hohfeld, *Fundamental Legal Conceptions as Applied in Judicial Reasoning*, (Westport 1978) for an analysis of the concepts right, power, privilege, immunity, liability and disability.

Underneath this first level of highly abstract legal concepts, there is, like in the general conceptual scheme, a second level of (in comparison to the first level) more concrete (but within the legal system still rather abstract) concepts like contract, crime, negligence, tort, breach of contract, guilt and justification. The concepts of this level are either heavily modified non-legal concepts or are even produced entirely by the legal system. Like the ones in the general case, on the second level they are, in the context of the legal system, much less necessary. The consequence is: They are much more open for inner-systemic determination and interpretation in the process of adjudication. That means: The structural vagueness and contingency of these concepts open up the possibility to determine these concepts by legal rules up to the extreme of total invention which is not possible for the most abstract concepts of the legal system on the first level because these most abstract concepts have to keep up the connection to our general conceptual scheme, that is to the non-legal world. Otherwise there would be no connection between the general and the legal conceptual scheme.

We then have a third level of concepts in the law which are similar to the general scheme close to empirical sensations, e.g. concepts like car, tree, vine, house, street, city, body, banana, apple, tomato, blue, red, loud, heavy. The internal determination of these concepts by the norms of the legal system is, like in the general conceptual scheme, rather limited, but not totally impossible.

Finally, in law we also have a fourth level of very concrete concepts. These concepts are used very often in quite technical norms like norms of environmental, medical or economic law, e.g. the concepts of special chemical substances, of medical drugs, of investment market instruments. These concepts are quite open for legal determination. They can be determined either by experts in special sciences (e.g. in chemistry for chemical substances) or by the law itself, e.g. the determination of concepts like driving license, identity card, constituency etc.

We can summarise: The general four-level model of different abstraction and necessity can also be found in the law because the law cannot withdraw its special conceptual scheme totally or largely from the determining features of our general conceptual scheme with its epistemological and justificatory function like the conceptual schemes of mathematics or physics perhaps can do. The possibility of internal determination of the concepts is not uniform, but variable. While the most abstract legal concepts on the first level and the empirical concepts on the third level are not very open to inner-systematic determination by the law, the rather abstract and very concrete concepts on level two and four are quite open for inner-systemic determination by the law up to a total invention.

Conceptual scheme in general		Conceptual scheme of the law
(1) highly abstract level		
(2) rather highly abstract level	→	(1) highly abstract level in law
	↘	
		(2) rather highly abstract level
(3) medium level of abstraction	→	(3) medium level of abstraction
	↘	
(4) low level of abstraction	→	(4) low level of abstraction

7 What Is More Fundamental: Concepts or Norms/Judgments?

We have now reached the last, mainly theoretical question which operates on a meta-level and is decisive for the decision between normativism and conceptualism in legal theory: Was the revolutionary departure from the classical conceptual view justified? Are norms and judgments really more fundamental than concepts in law?

Alf Ross argued in his famous article entitled 'Tû-tû' that legal concepts, like ownership, can be reduced to the inferences between norms.[28] These legal concepts have no meaning in the sense of reference. They are nothing more than the sum of the rules which attach to them certain normative consequences. Ross tells a fictive story about a primitive tribe, where three events cause a person to become 'tû-tû': encountering his or her mother-in-law, eating from the chieftain's food or killing a totem animal. If a person has become tû-tû he or she must undertake a purification ceremony. Ross holds that the middle concept tû-tû has – if superstition about tû-tû is avoided – no meaning in the sense of reference. It can be justified only for reasons of abbreviation, that is, to connect different conditions of the norm with the ordering part of the norm, that is, the order to undertake the process of purification.

First of all, one has to realise that, with the concept of ownership, Alf Ross has (willingly or unwillingly) chosen a concept which is situated on the second general level of the general levels mentioned in the fifth section, the level which is quite open for inner-systematic determination by the legal rules. So Ross has made a point for this and similar concepts of the second general level in some respect.

But some severe limitations of his thesis have to be mentioned. *First*: Ross has only shown the possibility of a normative system which uses inner-systematic concepts for purely abbreviating purposes. He has not, however, shown their actuality, that is, that one, many or even all actual legal concepts in actual legal systems have to be understood as only serving such an inferential function.

Second: Ross only mentions a few concepts like 'right', 'duty', 'territory', 'claim'. The result for these concepts cannot be generalised to all or only the main legal concepts. Ross does not claim such a generalization explicitly. It does not hold for concepts of the first general level, the third level, and many concepts of the fourth level: Additionally, the concepts of the first level of the legal order like human being, action or punishment are mainly taken from outside the law and connect the law with our non-legal understanding of the world, so they cannot be replaced totally by legal norms. The concepts of the third level of the legal order, like 'tree', 'bird' or 'dog', can only be understood with reference to sense experiences. They are not purely legally determined. The concepts of the fourth level, like Golden Delicious or Boskop, are open for inner-systematic determination in general. But often external

---

28 Alf Ross, 'Tû-Tû', 70 *Harvard Law Review* (1956/1957), 812–825. See for an analysis of middle terms: Lars Lindahl, 'Deduction and Justification in the Law. The Role of Legal Terms and Concepts', 17 *Ratio Juris* (2004) 182–202. See also: Lothar Philipps, 'Tû-Tû 2. Von Rechtsbegriffen und neuronalen Netzen' in Lothar Philipps and Roland Wittmann (eds.), *Rechtsentstehung und Rechtskultur* (Heidelberg 1991), Giovanni Sartor, *Understanding and Applying Legal Concepts: An Inquiry on Inferential Meaning* and Jaap Hage, *The Meaning of Legal Status Words*, both in this volume.

determinations will be decisive, e.g. the different sorts of apples, because of pragmatic reasons, cannot be changed by legal norms totally.

Third: Even for such rather abstract and technical legal concepts like ownership, right, claim or territory, Ross overestimates the dependence of the concept on rules and underestimates the dependence of the concept from other concepts. It is, for example, clear that the concept of ownership is not only shaped by the rules which attach normative consequences to it, but also by more abstract concepts like subjective right, and more concrete concepts like ownership of immovable and movable things, or ownership of corporal and non-corporal things – if this is acknowledged by a legal system.[29] For example if one thinks that ownership of non-corporal things is possible, the relation between owner and owned thing cannot be a purely physical relation.

Fourth: Even such a juridical term like ownership has some factual (that is, natural and social/institutional) counterpart in the world, like a physical or mental relationship between person and thing and a form of generally accepted power over things, that is, social facts.[30] Ross doesn't try to identify this factual counterpart. His analysis of the concept of ownership, therefore, is incomplete. The tû-tû-example is, in this respect, self-defeating, due to the fact that it works only because the view of the Indians and the missionary are not taken separately, but instead combined. The Indians assume that the word 'tû-tû' has some corresponding real state of affairs, and, therefore, is not meaningless. If they would acquire the view of the missionary that the belief in tû-tû is pure superstition, they would immediately abandon the norm to undertake a purification ceremony after becoming tû-tû, because if the conditions of encountering the mother-in-law, eating from the chieftain's food or killing a totem animal are no longer believed to lead to the state of affair of tû-tû, the undertaking of a purification ceremony is no longer necessary. This shows that the concept tû-tû has not only an inferential function, but, for the Indians, it also refers to a state of affairs which justifies that the purification process shall take place. If one were to insert 'old cheese' in the purification-norm – a proposal by Ross – instead of 'tû-tû', there would be no norm-independent justification for the purification process any more. For concepts like ownership, the situation is similar. Ownership is believed by the people as a justified factual close relationship between persons and things including a factual power to preserve this relationship, e.g. in archaic societies most people have most of the things they own attached to their bodies (clothes, glasses and so on) or in their houses (furniture, weapons, kitchen utensils). If this factual relationship and this factual power did not occur in reality, there would be no reason to issue the normative consequences which are normally associated with property, like the right to restitution in cases of theft, or the right to compensation in cases of damages by others.

Fifth: Ross follows nominalism (by the way without any discussion) and thinks that concepts are words. And he considers only the semantic function of reference or

[29] The German system does exclude this: § 90 BGB: 'Sachen sind nur körperliche Gegenstände.'
[30] See the critique of Jaap Hage, *The Meaning of Legal Status Words*.

extension (Bedeutung). So he assumes a rather reduced understanding of meaning, one which dismisses intentions (Sinn).[31] He does not take into account other functions of concepts, especially their epistemological function and their evaluative, that is, justificatory, function.

This brings us back to the aim of this article, the attack on normativism in legal theory via a fundamental justification as to why normativism is an unjustified reductionism and why, in addition to norms, rules or principles, concepts play such a crucial role in legal reasoning. This most fundamental justification, stated in section 2, is the defence of conceptualism that is the understanding of concepts as mental representations which are decisive for our understanding of the world and the critique of nominalism that is the unjustified reduction of concepts to words or connections of words.

8 Conclusion

Our inquiry has shown that concepts are decisive and even more fundamental than norms for a legal system. So normativism is not justified in general. Therefore, conceptual analysis is crucial for legal reasoning, although there might be differences from legal system to legal system and within one legal system. Roman law and its reception, for example, produced a lot more quite abstract and technical concepts earlier than the Common law did. And in civil and penal law, specific technical concepts seem to play a more important role than in constitutional and administrative law, because the former legal fields are much older and much more carefully conceptualised than the latter. But a full understanding of the status of concepts in law would have to inquire into how the formation and interpretation of legal concepts work in different legal systems and different parts of the law.

[31] Alf Ross, *Tû-Tû*, 820.

Understanding and Applying Legal Concepts: An Inquiry on Inferential Meaning

Giovanni Sartor

1 Legal Concepts and Legal Inferences

Legal concepts are typically encountered in the context of legal norms, and the issue of determining their content cannot be separated from the issue of identifying and interpreting (or constructing) the norms in which they occur, and of using such norms in legal inference. Consequently, it can be argued that a legal system endows its concepts with meaning exactly by embedding such concepts (the terms expressing them) within certain legal norms. Rather than assuming that legal terms have a prior independent meaning, according to which we should determine the meaning of the norms containing them, we should focus on the norms containing such terms and on the inferences they enable, and consequently determine the conceptual contents that such terms are meant to convey. This is particularly the case for the so-called 'intermediate legal concepts,' namely, those concepts through which legal norms convey both legal consequences and preconditions of further legal effects, as we shall see in the following. These are indeed the concepts whose semantics we want to investigate, and to which we shall refer when speaking of 'legal concepts' *tout court*.

This inferential understanding of the meaning of legal concepts corresponds to the idea that legal norms basically work as 'inference rules': they tell the legal reasoner what legal conclusions (an obligation, a permission, a right, a normative qualification, a status etc.) he or she should derive given certain preconditions. Using Frank Ramsey's terminology we may say that legal norms are *variable*

G. Sartor (✉)
European University Institute of Florence, Florence, Italy
e-mail: giovanni.sartor@eui.eu

This contribution refines and develops ideas I presented in a previous work, where the inferential model was compared to approaches based on the idea that terminological definitions can distinguished from the substantive legal rules: Giovanni Sartor, 'The Nature of Legal Concepts: Inferential Nodes or Ontological Categories', in: Gianmaria Ajani, Giovanni Sartor, and Daniela Tiscornia (eds.), *Proceeding of the Conference on 'Approaching the Multilanguage Complexity of European Law: Methodologies in Comparison'* (Florence 2007).

J.C. Hage, D. von der Pfordten (eds.), *Concepts in Law*, Law and Philosophy Library 88,
DOI 10.1007/978-90-481-2982-9_3, © Springer Science+Business Media B.V. 2009

hypotheticals,[1] namely, informational structures that are 'rules for judging', as according to the pattern 'If I meet a ϕ, I shall regard it as a ψ.' Such general conditionals are often called simply *rules* but I prefer to use the term *inferential link*, since in the legal domain the term *rule* has a variety of meanings that are not relevant to the present analysis (for instance the concept of a rule is often associated with the idea of the command of a ruler, or with the idea of an obligation, or with the idea of an 'exclusionary reason').[2] Here I will only consider legal rules, but it may be useful to clarify that the notion of an inferential link is broader than the idea of a legal norm, since it can be applied to moral norms and to non-normative connections (such as the relation between causes and effects or between symptoms and causes).[3]

The idea of norms as inferential links can be stretched to cover all legal norms, both conditional and nonconditional ones: nonconditional norms can be viewed degenerate inferential links having no antecedent, so that their content (their 'conclusion') can immediately be endorsed by the reasoner, without the need of checking for preconditions. However, this idea – by focusing on the conditional relation between a link's antecedents and its conclusion – directly corresponds to the widespread view that legal norms typically have the conditional form:

IF condition (operative facts or *Tatbestand*) *THEN conclusion* (legal effect)

For instance, a trivially simplified representation of the concept of Italian citizenship can be provided by two sets of inferential links, the links leading to the acquisition of the Italian citizenship

- *IF* x is born in Italy, *THEN* x is an Italian citizen
- *IF* x is born from Italian parents, *THEN* x is an Italian citizen
- ... (further ways of acquiring citizenship)

and the links establishing the consequences of Italian citizenship

---

[1] Frank Plumpton Ramsey, *The Foundations of Mathematics and Other Essays*, Richard Bevan Braithwaite (ed.) (London 1931), 241.

[2] As in the terminology of Joseph Raz, *Practical Reason and Norms* (London 1975). In computing, on the contrary, the term *rule* is usually employed to denote any conditional structures. For instance we speak of *rule-based systems* to refer to computer systems containing and using information represented in conditional form.

[3] I am using the terms *normative proposition* and a *norm* as synonyms. I do not follow the terminology of Carlos Alchourrón and Eugenio Bulygin, for whom a normative proposition is a meta-level assertion concerning what can or cannot be deduced from a given set of norms. See Carlos E. Alchourròn and Eugenio Bulygin, *Normative Systems,* (Vienna 1971). The idea that (conditional) norms can be primarily viewed as inferential links (rather than, for instance, as imperatives) is connected to the view that norms are information structures having a specific role in practical cognition, i.e., in the process though which a (boundedly) rational agent evaluates and selects actions. See Giovanni Sartor, *Legal Reasoning: A Cognitive Approach to the Law,* vol. 5, Treatise on Legal Philosophy and General Jurisprudence, Enrico Pattaro (ed.) (Berlin 2005).

- *IF* x is an Italian citizen, *THEN* x has the right to stay in Italy
- *IF* x is an Italian citizen and x is of full age, *THEN* x has the right to vote in Italian elections
- ... (further consequences of citizenship).

If the law is primarily constituted by a set of inferential links, then concepts – and in particular lexical concepts, namely, the concepts corresponding to the words or syntagms of a language – seem to play a dependent semantic role.[4] In fact, legal inferences concern whole sentences (antecedent and consequent sentences connected through inferential links), and as a result lexical terms are not primary carriers of meaning.[5] Rather, it seems that the meaning of a term results from the set of inferential links concerning the sentences in which the term occurs: these inferences constitute the mean of the corresponding concept, and changes in the normative network immediately determine conceptual changes. For instance the concept of citizenship may be seen as emerging from the set of inferential links establishing what preconditions (birth in Italy, having Italian parents, and so on) determine citizenship and what further consequences are entailed by this qualification (permission to stay in Italy, the right to vote, etc.).

2 Ross' Theory of Legal Concepts

The idea that legal rules (viewed as inferential links of the type just described) determine, and even exhaust, the meaning of legal concepts was advanced by Alf Ross,[6] who imagines a population, the Noît-cif tribe, endorsing two kinds of links:

1. links stating under what conditions something is (or starts to be) tû-tû, and
2. links stating what normative qualifications or positions are determined by having or acquiring the tû-tû quality.

[4] The term *concept* is here used in the most general sense, namely as referring to any content associated to a linguistic expression. This most general notion of a *concept* should be distinguished from specific and more restricted ways of using the term *concept*, as in description logics (and other formal theories of knowledge representation), where *concepts* are understood as monadic predicates, denoting a class of individuals, to the exclusion of binary relationships, which are called properties or *roles*. See Daniele Nardi and Ronald J. Bratman, 'An Introduction to Description Logics', in: Franz Baader et al. (eds.), *Description Logic Handbook* (Cambridge, Mass. 2002) 5–44.

[5] This view was advanced by Gottlob Frege, who affirmed that 'it is only in the context of a proposition that words have any meaning' (Gottlob Frege, *The Basic Laws of Arithmetic* (Berkley 1964) 73), though there is a vast discussion in the Frege literature concerning whether he has abandoned the 'context-principle' in his later works. This principle has been endorsed among the others by William Quine, according to whom 'sentences and not words' are 'the wholes whose use is learned' (Willard Van Orman Quine, *World and Object (*Cambridge, Mass. 1960) 1). On the extraction of sub-sentential meaning from sentential inferences, see Robert Brandom, *Making It Explicit: Reasoning, Representing, and Discursive Commitment* (Cambridge, Mass. 1994). For criticism, see Jerry Fodor and Ernie Lepore, 'Brandom's Burdens: a review of Robert B. Brandom's Articulating Reasons', in: *Philosophy and Phenomenological Research* 63 (2001), 465–482.

[6] Alf Ross, 'Tû-Tû', in: *Scandinavian Studies in Law* 1 (1957), 139–153.

These two types of links are exemplified[7] by the following rules:

- *IF* one has eaten of the chief's food, *THEN* one is tû-tû;
- *IF* one is tû-tû, *THEN* one shall be subjected to a ceremony of purification.

According to Ross, to understand how the word *tû-tû* is used by the Noît-cifonians we need only to gather all links of the two kinds just mentioned, that is, all links establishing the following:

1. when someone or something qualifies as tû-tû, or
2. what further normative qualifications or positions are determined by having the tû-tû quality.

Note that the Noît-cifonian population endorses both kinds of links: those concerning the determination of the tû-tû quality (for instance, rules stating that killing a totemic animal determines the killer's tû-tû-ness, or that meeting one's mother-in-law determines one's tû-tû-ness), and those concerning the effects determined by tû-tû-ness (for instance, rules stating that tû-tû-ness determines the prohibition of participating in certain ritual activities, or the obligation to undergo a purification ceremony). We thus get the normative information represented in Fig. 1, where each arrow-connection represents a general rule.

For instance the arrow between 'x eats of the chief's food' and 'x is tû-tû' stands for the rule

FORANY (x) *IF* x eats of the chief's food *THEN* x is tû-tû

The members of the tribe perform two inferential steps for obtaining deontic conclusions (for inferring permissions or obligations) in tû-tû matters: the first step is concerned with establishing that someone or something is tû-tû (according to links concerning tû-tû's initiation), and the second step is concerned with establishing a deontic implication of tû-tû-ness (according to links establishing tû-tû's effects).

According to this characterisation, Tû-tû appears to be an *intermediate legal concept*, located between its (factual) preconditions and its (deontic) conclusions, and whose conceptual function consists indeed in mediating such preconditions and

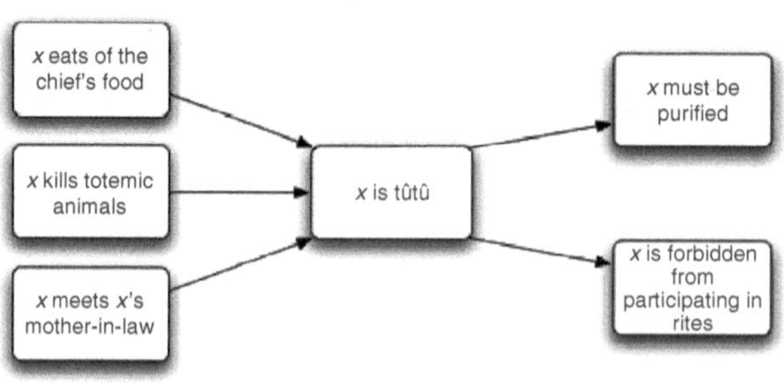

Fig. 1 Tû-tû, an intermediate normative concept

[7] Ross, *Tû-Tû*.

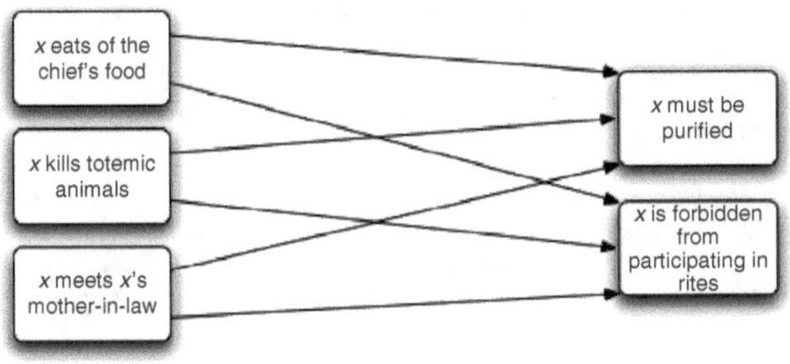

Fig. 2 Elimination of tû-tû

conclusions.[8] Consequently, Ross argues that the tû-tû concept is superfluous, in the sense that the same deontic conclusions licensed by tû-tû-based inferences can equally be obtained through inferences directly connecting facts and deontic qualifications. If the members of the tribe were to disremember the tû-tû links and learn the links in Fig. 2, they would not lose any real normative information: they would still be able to derive, given the same factual preconditions, the same deontic conclusions they could previously obtain (when they were still operating under the tû-tû links).

According to the new links of Fig. 2, these conclusions would be derived in one step, for instance directly jumping from the fact that Tom ate the chief's food to the conclusion that Tom must be purified, without passing through the intermediate conclusion that Tom is tû-tû.

Ross claims that non-deontic legal qualifications, such as the notion of ownership, are logically not different from tû-tû-ness: their function is limited to connecting factual preconditions and normative effects, as one can see in Fig. 3.

Like tû-tû-ness, so ownership can be eliminated without deontic loss, simply by substituting the set of links in Fig. 2, with the set in Fig. 3. The result we obtain by eliminating ownership is a more complex knowledge representation: in Fig. 4

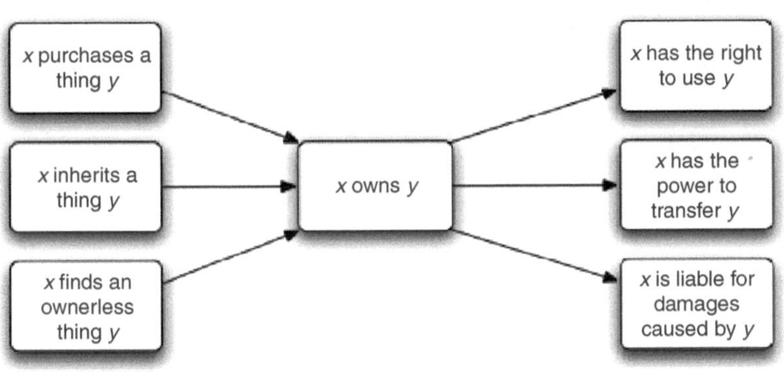

Fig. 3 Ownership, an intermediate legal concept

[8] Though Ross does not use the term *intermediate legal concept*, this term has been often used in the subsequent literature referring to his work, see for instance, Lars Lindahl and Jan Odelstad, 'An Algebraic Analysis of Normative Systems', in: *Ratio Juris* 13 (2000), 261–278.

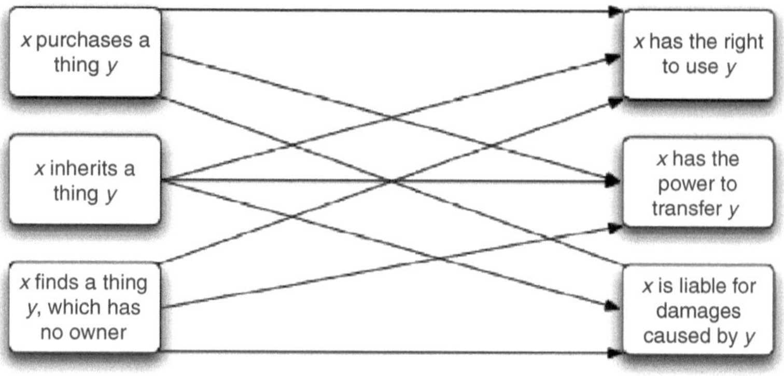

Fig. 4 The elimination of ownership

we have nine connections, that is, nine links rather than the six links of Fig. 3.[9] However, as Ross correctly remarks, by eliminating ownership in this way – through a conceptual revision of all the original ownership-based links – we preserve the possibility of inferring the same deontic conclusions in the same factual situations.

From this indubitable fact, so clearly stated, Ross comes at questionable conclusions. In particular, he makes the following claim:

> [T]he 'ownership' inserted between the conditioning facts and the conditioned consequences is in reality a meaningless word without any semantic reference whatever, serving solely as a means of presentation.[10]

Therefore, Ross's view of the function of intermediate legal concepts – they enable us to simplify the representation of normative information – leads Ross to a radical conclusion concerning the semantics of these concepts: they are just meaningless dummies.

This seems to me rather excessive. In fact, we need to reformulate our links, so as to eliminate the concept of ownership all the while preserving the same normative consequences. This shows that the term *ownership* did have a meaning after all, in

---

[9] As Lars Lindhal observes, ideas similar to Ross's were advanced about the same time by Anders Wedberg (Lars Lindahl, 'Operative and Justificatory Grounds in Legal Argumention', in: *Associations* 7 (2003), 185–200, 193f.). According to Wedberg, the use of 'meaningless expressions' has the function – not only in the law, but also in the natural science – of reducing the number of links that are needed to license certain conclusions (Anders Wedberg, 'Some Problems in the Logical Analysis of Legal Science', in: *Theoria* 17 (1951), 246–275).

When we have m sentences $A_1 \ldots A_m$ and n sentences $B_1 \ldots B_n$ in order to be able to infer from each A_i all of the $B_1 \ldots B_n$, we have two choices. The first choice consists in having, for each A_i, n links connecting A_i to each of the $B_1 \ldots B_n$. This implies having m^*n links altogether (this is the situation we have represented in Figs. 2 and 4. The second choice consists in introducing 'a meaningless symbol Z' having the following links: (a) for each A_i, one link connecting A_i to Z, and (b) for each B_j, one link connecting Z to B_j. This implies having only $m + n$ links overall, a number of links much smaller than $m^a stn$ (when m and n grow large enough), as one can see by comparing Figs. 1 and 3 to Figs. 2 and 4. For a recent discussion of Ross's approach see also Bob Brouwer and Jaap Hage 'Fundamental Concepts of European Private Law', in: *European Review of Private Law* 1 (2007).

[10] Ross, *Tû-Tû*.

the sense that it played a conceptual role: the reformulation is required exactly to express in a different way the legal contents we previously expressed by relaying on the term's conceptual role.[11] With regard to terms expressing legal qualifications, we could thus say that such terms have an *inferential meaning*. The *meaning* of a legal qualification Q – intended as Q's *conceptual function* – is given by two sets of inferential links:

a. the links stating what conditions determine the qualification Q (Q-conditioning links), and
b. the links connecting further properties to possession of the qualification Q (Q-conditioned links).

The connection between meaning and inferences enables us to derive two corollaries. First, Q-conditioning and Q-conditioned links *constitute* Q's inferential meaning, since they determine what inferences lead to Q and what inferences depart from it. For instance, we can say that:

a. ownership-conditioning links contribute to constituting the notion of ownership by establishing that ownership is acquired under certain conditions, while
b. ownership-conditioned links contribute to constituting the notion of ownership by establishing the rights and duties of owners.

Secondly, such links determine whether Q applies to particular individual entities and what further properties Q-qualified entities have. Therefore, these links *constitute* the fact that certain individuals are Q's, as well as they constitute the normative consequences of this fact. For instance, we can say that:

a. ownership-conditioning links contribute to constituting the fact that current owners own certain things, by having enabled the normative generation of their ownership of those things (as resulting from the conditions determining ownership according to such links), while
b. ownership-conditioned links contribute to constituting current owners' rights and obligations, by providing for the normative generation of the normative entitlements owners have with regard to their possessions (as resulting, according to such links, from their ownership of these possessions).

Hence inferential links have a double legal significance: on the one hand they determine legal meanings and on the other hand they determine legal state of affairs and consequential effects. These two aspects are necessarily interdependent: any

[11] In general, the fact that we can transform a theory T_1 using term t into a theory T_2 that does not use term t, but has the same implications of $T1$ (with regard to statements not containing t) does not prove that t is meaningless, but rather that we can conceptualise a certain domain in different equivalent ways (the issue will then be what way is simpler, more elegant, more helpful for a certain inquiry). It is indeed very common especially in formal disciplines (like logic, game theory, etc.) that equivalent systems can be provided, which use different terms, defined in different ways.

choice concerning the meaning of legal terms amounts to a choice concerning legal effects.

3 Implications of an Inferential Theory of Legal Concepts

The idea that legal concepts have an inferential semantics has some interesting implications. A first implication consists in questioning (at least when all inferential links are treated equally) the distinction between terminological information (word knowledge) and substantive information (world knowledge), and consequently in eliminating the distinction between linguistic (analytic) and legal (synthetic) information.[12] If the meaning of legal words were defined independently of inferential links (as provided by substantive legal norms), then we could separately consider what meaning a legal word has, and what norms are expressed using that word. If, on the contrary, norms constitute meanings, such a distinction becomes much more blurred. We could try to distinguish, among the inferential links pertaining to a certain term, those links which constitute the meaning of the term, and those which do not constitute such meaning (but only provide information about the referent of the concept), but it seems very difficult to provide precise general criteria for operating such a distinction.[13] We can obviously distinguish conceptual and substantive information in ways that are appropriate to certain practical purposes, like constructing a dictionary, a taxonomy, or a set of legislative definitions, but it seems difficult to go beyond that.

A second implication of the view that legal meanings are determined by inferential connections consists in the fact that legal concepts are determined by legal systems: since each legal norm using a concept contributes to characterising the meaning of that concept, and different legal norms exist in different legal systems, then different systems have different concepts.[14]

---

[12] According to a long tradition (extending from Leibniz and Kant to logical empiricism), the truth-value of an analytical judgment is determined exclusively by the meaning of the terms occurring in it. A synthetic judgment, by contrast, says something that is not included in the meaning of such terms. 'Bachelors are unmarried men' is a classical example of an analytic judgment, while 'Bachelors take longer holidays' is an example of a synthetic judgments, whose truth-value depends not only on the concepts used but also on the states of affairs in the world. The distinction between analytic and synthetic judgments, famously criticised by Quine (see Willard Van Orman Quine, 'Two Dogmas of Empiricism', in: *The Philosophical Review* 60 (1951), 20–43; 2nd revised edition in *The Logical Point of View* (Cambridge, Mass. 1961)), has been recently proposed again in new forms. See, for instance, Paul Boghossian, 'Analyticity', in: Bob Hale and Crispin Wright (eds.), *A Companion to the Philosophy of Language* (Oxford 1997) 331–368.

[13] On the idea that legal terms have a core meaning covering some, but not necessarily all of their inferential features, see Uberto Scarpelli, *Contributo alla semantica del linguaggio normativo* (Milan 1959) and Anna Pintore, *La teoria analitica dei concetti giuridici* (Naples 1990) 130f.

[14] For a discussion of conceptual diversity, see, for instance, Gianmaria Ajani and Martin Ebers, 'Uniform Terminology for European Contract Law: Introduction', in: Gianmaria Ajani and Martin Ebers (eds.), *Uniform Terminology for European Contract Law* (Baden-Baden 2005) 11–20.

A third implication is that legal semantics is determined (among other things) by legal doctrine, to the extent that doctrine determines, identifies or constructs legal norms on the basis of the sources of law. According to the inferential approach, the discussion concerning the meaning of a legal concept in a legal system concerns establishing what inferential links – leading to, or departing from, the term expressing the concept – hold in that system. Since the inferential links holding in a legal system represent, or are derivable from, norms of such a system, this discussion is inseparable from the doctrinal issues concerning what legal norms belong to a legal system (given the available legal material, such as legislation, precedent, custom, and so on) and consequently constitute correct premises of legal reasoning with regard to that system. On the one hand, when we argue that in a given legal system certain preconditions determine the application of a concept and that certain consequences follow from it, we are arguing that such inferential links correspond to norms of such a system. On the other hand, when we consider whether a certain norm exists in a legal system we must take into account the conceptual network in which the norm participates: if the norm links a conceptual qualification to certain preconditions, we must consider what consequences other norms connect to that qualification; if the norm provides consequences of a certain conceptual qualification, we must consider what preconditions entail this qualification.

In fact, by constructing in a certain way (through doctrinal interpretation/construction) the inferential links characterising a certain concept in a legal system we contribute to determining the substantive legal conclusions derivable according to that system. Consequently, we will argue for one or the other interpretative construction of the relevant inferential links according to what conclusions, derivable according to such links, we believe better fit (the values and principles we associate with) the considered legal system.

Consider, for instance, the recent debate about torture, where the absolute prohibition of torture[15] has been recently questioned with regard to the treatment of suspect terrorists.[16] A lawyer believing that the law permits infliction of pain on detainees for the purpose of extracting useful information has two ways to go about showing that this is the case: the lawyer can take either a restricted view of the conditions for applying the concept of torture (requiring, for instance, that permanent physical damage is caused, so as to exclude that there is torture when pain is inflicted without such an effect) or a restricted view of the consequences of qualifying an act as torture (assuming that only certain kinds of tortures are always forbidden, while other kinds of torture are in certain circumstances permissible). Correspondingly, a lawyer believing, on the contrary, that the law never permits any infliction of pain for the purpose of extracting information will claim that every pain inflicted for this purpose qualifies as torture, and will claim as well that the law prohibits every act of torture regardless of the form it may take. The two lawyers, in offering

---

[15] As stated in Art. 5 of the Universal Declaration of Human Rights: 'No one shall be subjected to torture or to cruel, inhuman or degrading treatment or punishment.'

[16] For a critical review of this debate, see Jeremy Waldron, 'Torture and Positive Law: Jurisprudence for the White House', in: *Columbia Law Review* 105 (2005), 1681–1746.

what they view as justified conditions for qualifying an act as torture or as justified consequences following from this qualification, will characterise in different ways the concept of torture, and this will have relevant deontic implications (the first characterisation of torture permits certain actions on detainees, actions which the second characterisation prohibits).

4 Inferential Meaning and Wrong Inferences

An inferential approach to the meaning of legal terms seems to entail that the understanding of legal concepts involves a *doctrinal commitment* with regard to the considered legal system (by a 'doctrinal commitment', I mean the belief that the considered legal system includes, or entails, certain particular normative contents). We can obviously make a doctrinally uncommitted use of the concept of torture by asserting that another person is using that concept in a certain way (which we may not share). However, when we frame in a certain way the very concept of torture we are using, we apparently take a stand on what counts as torture and on what normative consequences follow from this qualification in our legal system (or in any case, in the legal system we are considering). Every statement concerning what inferences can be derived from a certain legal concept, or what inferences lead to a legal concept, seems to become immediately a doctrinal commitment, namely, it seems to commit us to the view that the corresponding inferential links hold in the legal system we are considering.

This approach to the inferential meaning of a legal concept can be connected with the general view that having a concept entails (or consists in) the disposition to make certain substantive inferences. This idea has been developed in particular by Michael Dummett, who has offered a well-known example concerning the French word *boche*, used disparagingly during World War I to refer to the Germans: you call someone a 'boche' who is German – this forms the basis for calling that person a 'boche' – and being boche entails having certain negative qualities, such as being cruel. According to Dummet,[17] one has the concept of *boche* just in case one accepts the following inferential links (and is ready to reason accordingly):

- if x is German, then x is boche;
- if x is boche, then x is cruel.

One is wrong in having such a concept – as one is wrong in having similar disparaging concepts about other nationalities or ethnic or other groups – since this concept prompts us to make wrong inferences. In fact, combining the two inferential steps above (*German* ⇒ *boche* ⇒ *cruel*), the premise that one is German produces the conclusion that one is cruel. Such an inference is clearly wrong (it leads us in general to false conclusions), since most Germans are not particularly cruel (not more than people belonging to other ethnic groups).

---

[17] Michael Dummett, *Frege's Philosophy of Language* (New York 1973) 454.

Developing this viewpoint, Brandom says: 'The use of any concept or expression involves commitment to an inference from its grounds to its consequences of application. Critical thinkers, or merely fastidious ones, must examine their idioms to be sure that they are prepared to endorse and so defend the appropriateness of the material inferential commitments implicit in the concepts they employ.'[18]

Paul Boghossian[19] has criticised Dummett and Brandom's analysis arguing that we can possess a concept while failing to endorse its constitutive inferences so that, in particular, we can knowingly possess defective concepts (concepts we know to be constituted by wrong inferences). We may doubt whether Dummett and Brandom really mean to exclude (as Boghossian seems to assume) that one can knowingly possess (in the sense of understand) a defective concept, or whether they rather only exclude the committed use of such a concept. However, it seems that some qualifications are required for making an inferential approach to meaning consistent with the possibility of having defective concepts. For instance Dummett affirms that 'learning to use a statement of a given form involves... learning two things: the conditions under which one is justified in making the statement; and what constitutes acceptance of it, i.e., the consequences of accepting it'.[20] This idea of learning (in combination with the idea that learning the use of a concept means learning the use of the statements in which it occurs) seems indeed to entail that we should be at difficulty in grasping a concept we can never use in making justified assertions (or also a concept which we can only use in making negative assertions).

5 Inferential Meaning and Substantive Legal Beliefs

While I agree with Dummett and Brandom on the importance of an inferential understanding of (legal) concepts, I believe, following Boghossian, that an inferential theory of legal concepts cannot limit itself to a strong (committing) way of having a concept; it must also provide a weaker way of possessing conceptual inferences, a way not involving the acceptance of such inferences, namely, not involving the belief that the corresponding inferential links hold in the domain we are considering. Such a weaker kind of inferential understanding should enable us to knowingly possess defective concepts (concepts whose constitutive inferential links

---

[18] Brandom continues as follows: 'The proper question to ask in evaluating the introduction and evolution of a concept is not whether the inference embodied is one that is already endorsed, so that no new content is really involved, but rather whether the inference is one that ought to be endorsed. The problem with *boche* is not that once we explicitly confront the material inferential commitment that gives the term its content it turns out to be novel, but that it can then be seen to be indefensible and inappropriate, a commitment we cannot become entitled to'. See Robert Brandom, *Articulating Reasons: An Introduction to Inferentialism* (Cambridge, Mass. 2000).

[19] Paul Boghossian, 'Epistemic Analyticity: A Defense', in: Hans-Johann Glock, Kathrin Gluer, and Geert Keil (eds.), *Grazer Philosophische Studien, Fifty Years of Quine's Two Dogmas* (Amsterdam 2003) 15–35.

[20] Dummett, *Frege's Philosophy of Language,* 453.

we know to be wrong), or local concepts (concepts whose inferences we know to be applicable in certain contexts, but not in certain other).

For characterising this weaker kind of conceptual possession I shall first provide some examples, and then I shall attempt at constructing a general model.

Suppose that I am analysing different approaches to marriage and that I identify a view of marriage, let me call it *patriarchal marriage*, which is characterised by (i.e., the meaning of which is given by) the following inferential links:

- *IF* a couple goes through a marriage ceremony, *THEN* the two spouses are in the relation of patriarchal marriage, and
- *IF* two spouses are in the relation of patriarchal marriage, *THEN* the husband has power over his wife.

Suppose that these links fully constitute the meaning of the term *patriarchal marriage*, as I understand it, and that I am fully aware of that. (I know that the meaning of this term is constituted by such links). Consider now the following question. Does my knowledge of the meaning of term *patriarchal marriage* entail that whenever I know that a couple has gone through a marriage ceremony, I should conclude that the husband has power over his wife? The answer must be negative: while possessing the concept of patriarchal marriage and knowing that a marriage ceremony has taken place, I must be able to reject the conclusion that the husband has such power (since I reject the idea that, in my legal system, a marriage ceremony entails a legal situation having such consequences). This seems very reasonable, but it is incompatible with the view that knowing the meaning of a term (and thus 'having', in a sense, the concept corresponding to such a term) involves having, among the premises of our reasoning, the corresponding inferential links. We can know a concept, but refuse to draw the concept's conclusions (while believing that its antecedent preconditions hold).

The problem with regard to inferentially characterised concepts is that the preconditions for certain entities to be qualified as an instance of a concept do not logically entail the consequences following from such a qualification. The fact that a couple went through a marriage ceremony – this being the precondition for qualifying the couple as being linked by a patriarchal marriage – does not entail according to logic alone that the husband has power over the wife: for drawing this conclusion we need to make substantive assumptions, namely, we need to assume that the inferential links hold that characterise the concept of patriarchal marriage. But our possession of a concept should not force us to believe that the inferential links characterising that concept really obtain.

Let me introduce one further example to clarify this point. Suppose that the concept of *debt-bondage* (a legal institution quite common in ancient legal systems, and unfortunately still in use in some parts of the word) is defined by the following links:

- *IF* x fails to repay x's debt toward y, *THEN* x is under debt-bondage toward y until x's debt is extinguished;
- *IF* x is under debt-bondage toward y, *THEN* x is bound to serve y.

Suppose that I grasp (and thus, in this sense, possess) this concept and that I know that Tom did not repay his debt toward Laura. Should I conclude that Tom is bound to serve Laura? This conclusion seems absurd: I can consistently possess the concept of debt-bondage and deny that its constitutive links hold and consequently reject the concept's consequences, even when its preconditions are satisfied. In fact, I need to possess a concept even for rejecting it, in the sense of declaring that it does not apply.

6 Ramsey's Elimination and Carnap's Conditionalisation of Theoretical Concepts

Paul Boghossian[21] has proposed a solution to the puzzle of defective concepts, referring to some ideas originally developed by Frank Ramsey and Rudolf Carnap. In the following I will adapt these ideas to legal concepts, and consequently I will extend Boghossian's solution to the legal domain. This will enable us to distinguish the mere understanding of a legal concept from the commitment to its applicability.

Ramsey developed the idea that theoretical concepts can be removed from scientific theories, but in a way different from the way in which Ross eliminated legal concepts: according to Ramsey theoretical terms can be replaced by variables.[22] By a *theoretical term* Ramsey means a term occurring in scientific theories, which applies to non-observable entities, like mass, energy, or proton. We can apply his idea also to intermediate legal concepts (terms), since they also concern qualifications that are not empirically observable: as theoretical terms in science are used within theories that connect (in complex ways) possible empirical data and forecasts of further empirical observations, so intermediate legal concepts are used within normative systems which connect (in complex ways) observable facts and normative qualifications of human actions.

Thus, given a theory (which for simplicity we can assume to consist of inferential links of the kind described above) containing a certain theoretical term, we can substitute that term with an existentially quantified variable. This substitution makes the assumption explicit that there exists some predicate that, substituted for the variable, yields true or valid propositions.[23]

---

[21] Boghossian, *Epistemic Analyticity: A Defense*.

[22] This idea was put forward in the paper 'Theories', written in 1929 and published posthumously in 1931. See Frank Plumpton Ramsey, *On Truth: Original Manuscript Materials, 1927–1929 from the Ramsey Collection at the University of Pittsburg*,(Dordrecht 1991).

[23] In general, given a theory T containing a term C, representing a theoretical concept, that is, denoting a non-observable category (a property or relation), we do the following: (a) we substitute C with a variable Z in all statements of T, obtaining a result that we denote as $T[C/Z]$, and (b) we specify that Z is existentially quantified. Thus, Ramsey's version of T is $(Z)(T[C/Z])$, where (Z) is to be read as 'there exists a Z such that'. For expediency, I will assume here that there is just one theoretical concept.

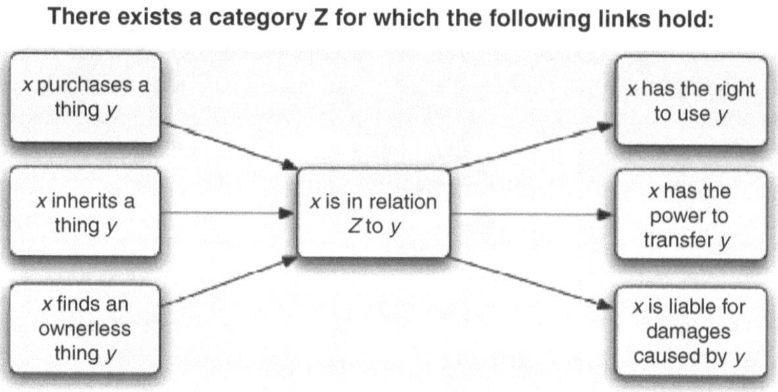

Fig. 5 The Ramseyfication of ownership

For instance, a Ramseyfied version of the inferential theory of the concept of ownership consists in the claim that *there exists a category* Z, which is characterised by the following inferential links (see Fig. 5):

- *IF* x buys a thing y, *THEN* x is in relation Z to y,
- *IF* x inherits a thing y, *THEN* x is in relation Z to y,
- ..., and
- *IF* x is in relation Z to y, *THEN* x can use y,
- *IF* x is in relation Z to y, *THEN* x can transfer y,
- ...

Ramsey points out that by substituting theoretical terms with existentially quantified variables no observable consequences of the original theory are lost (assuming that the theory provides all the inferences concerning the theoretical terms at issue).

Note that if possessing a concept amounted to accepting the Ramseyfied version of the theory characterising that concept, then possessing a legal concept would amount to accepting substantive legal claims. Having a concept would not only consist in understanding an idea, but would also amount to claiming that this idea has concrete reality, namely, that there exists a category for which the concept's constitutive inferences really obtain. For instance, possessing a concept of patriarchal marriage would entail assuming that there exists (in the context of the legal system we are considering) a relation Z having the following inferential features: (*a*) if a couple goes though a marriage ceremony, they are in this relation Z, and (*b*) if a couple is in the relation Z, then the husband has power over the wife. The existence of the category entails the holding of its inferential links. On the contrary, it seems to me that I can possess the concept of a patriarchal marriage – and use it, at least in negative or meta-level assertions, like when asserting that x and y are not linked by patriarchal marriage, or that this kind of marriage involves the husband's supremacy – without assuming that the inferential links constitutive of such a concept hold in the legal domain. We need to distinguish the possession of a concept, from the belief that the concept's constitutive links obtain.

To clarify this distinction we can adopt an idea advanced by Rudolf Carnap.[24] This is the idea is that a concept's possession can be expressed through a conditional sentence having the following content: if there exists some category satisfying the concept's inferential links, then these links hold with regard the concept at issue. In other words, the Carnap sentence says that if there exists a category (a property or relation) satisfying the concept's inferential links, then we may assume that this is the same category as denoted by the name of our concept, and we may consequently apply to this category the corresponding inferential links. [25]

For instance, Carnap's statement about patriarchal marriage would be something like the following:

if there exists a category Z such that

- *IF* a couple goes though a marriage ceremony, *THEN* they are in this relation Z, and
- *IF* a couple is in relation Z, *THEN* the husband has power over the wife

then

- *IF* a couple goes though a marriage ceremony, *THEN* they are in relation *patriarchal marriage*, and
- *IF* a couple is in relation *patriarchal marriage*, *THEN* the husband has power over the wife

7 Possession of Legal Concepts and Belief in Their Applicability

It seems to me that the possession of a concept is given by the acceptance of the corresponding Carnap sentence: I possess the concept of patriarchal marriage if I believe that, in case there exists (in the context I am considering) a category having the inferential features proper to patriarchal marriage (a marriage ceremony entails this relation, which entails husband's power), then these inferential features do indeed characterise the concept of patriarchal marriage. This way of possessing the concept of patriarchal marriage does not force me to conclude that husbands have power over their wives with regard to legal systems where this is not the case: I can draw such a conclusion only with regard to a legal system where a relation exists having all the inferential properties of patriarchal marriage, namely, where it

---

[24] See Stathis Psillos, Rudolf Carnap's 'Theoretical Concepts in Science', in: *Studies in History and Philosophy of Science* 31 (2000), 151–72. This contribution contains the text of a hitherto unpublished lecture delivered by Carnap on 1959.

[25] Let us assume that *TC* is our original theory containing term C, and let us denote the corresponding Ramsey statement (the Ramseyfication of theory *TC*) as $(X)(TC[C/X])$, abbreviated as TC_R (so that TC_R means that there exists a X such that we obtain a true theory by substituting term 'C' with 'X', namely, by assuming that C denotes that particular X). The corresponding Carnap statement (or rather, a simplified version of it) would then be $TC_R \Rightarrow TC$ (meaning that if the Ramsey statement holds then also the original theory holds).

is the case that a (successful) marriage ceremony brings about a relation between husband and wife entailing the husband's power.

Unless I assume that all of these entailments do hold in the legal system I am considering, my understanding (possession) of the concept of patriarchal marriage does not commit me to the sexist conclusion at issue. The possession of the concept is even compatible with the view that nowhere husbands have a legal power over their wives (this being in conflict with prevailing universal human rights[26]): according to this view the possessed concept will nowhere be applicable, since its constitutive inferential links nowhere hold. However, such a defective concept may still be useful, for instance, in order to argue that it is indeed inapplicable, or to argue that somebody (wrongly) believes that it is applicable.

We can then distinguish the mere *possession* of an inferentially characterised concept from the *belief in its applicability* to a certain context, namely, the belief that the concept can be used, according to its constitutive inferences, in that context.[27]

My possessing (in the sense of understanding or grasping) a concept requires only that I accept the corresponding Carnap sentence, namely, that I believe the following proposition: if there exists a category having the inferential links of the concept, then the concept's inferential links obtain. For instance, I possess the concept of patriarchal marriage in case I have the following belief: if there exists a relation having the inferential features of patriarchal marriage, then the term *patriarchal marriage* applies to this relation and the corresponding inferences hold with regard to this term.

My *belief in the applicability* of a concept requires an addition to its mere possession: besides accepting the Carnap sentence, I need to accept as well the corresponding Ramsey sentence, that is, I need to believe that a category exists such that the inferential features of the concept obtain with regard to that category: only if such a category exists the inferences constituting the concept will produce true (justified) conclusions. By combining the Ramsey sentence (an appropriate category exists) with the Carnap sentence (if an appropriate category exists, then the concept's inferences obtain), I can conclude that the concept's inferences actually obtain: given the Carnap sentence $TC_R \Rightarrow TC$ and the Ramsey sentence TC_R I can infer TC. Thus, in order to believe that the concept of patriarchal marriage is applicable to a certain context, I need to believe that there exists in that context a relation generated by marriage that gives the husband power over his wife (the content of this belief is my Ramsey sentence), a relation that (according to the corresponding Carnap sentence) I will identify as patriarchal marriage. Only if such a category exists, the concept will be applicable to the normative system I am considering.

---

[26] In particular with Art. 16 of the Universal Declaration of Human Rights, stating that men and women 'are entitled to equal rights as to marriage, during marriage and at its dissolution.'

[27] As the editors of this volume, Jaap Hage and Dietmar von der Pfordten have kindly remarked to me, the idea that a concept may fail to apply to a situation can also be found in Wittenstein's Tractatus, where it is said that 'In a proposition a situation is, at it were, constructed by way of experiment', meaning that such an experiment can fail (Ludwig Wittgenstein, *Tractatus Logico-Philosophicus* (London 1922) par. 4.031).

The most permissive condition for a concept to identify an existing inferential category can be extracted from the characterisation of the concept itself: if a concept is meant to bridge its preconditions and its conclusion, the category will exist whenever there is the possibility of building such a bridge, namely when each precondition of the concept determines all of the concept's consequences. Thus the category identified by the intermediate concept Z (for example, *x owns y*) will exist with regard to a certain context Γ only if each precondition of Z (for example, *x purchases y*) determines, with regard to Γ, all consequences derivable from Z (*x has the right to use y,...*).

More precisely, let concept Z be inferentially characterised as being entailed by each precondition A_i in $A_1 \ldots A_m$ and entailing all consequences $B_1 \ldots B_n$. We can say that a category **Z** corresponding to concept Z exists with regard to the normative systems Γ only if each precondition A_1 of Z entails with regard to Γ the conjunction $B_1 \ldots B_n$ (namely, if Γ does not entail $B_1 \ldots B_n$, but $\Gamma \cup A_i$ does). When this condition is satisfied, we can also say that concept Z is applicable to Γ. In other words a concept is applicable to Γ, if according to Γ each case satisfying one of Z's preconditions also satisfies (or normally satisfies, in case of defeasible entailment) all of Z's consequences.

The mere applicability of a concept (namely, the existence of the corresponding category, in the sense just specified) does not imply that the concept has cognitive value and thus deserves to be explicitly recognised and denoted by a specific term. A concept deserves such a recognition only to the extent that it collects a set of inferential links whose collection is cognitively useful, since it reflects the nature of the domain to be examined. Within the epistemology of natural sciences, it has been said that concepts should approximate *generals* or *real types*, meant as 'clusters of properties co-occurring because they are lawfully connected'.[28] Consider for instance the properties that are associated with the concept of gold, which can be explained by the physical laws which depend upon gold's atomic structure. In the same way, a legal concept should unify a bundle of normative links sharing not only the same legal effects, but also the same normative justification.[29] This should ensure the persistency and the cognitive relevance of the bundle so identified. For instance, the concept of ownership unifies a set of operative facts – the different ways of acquiring ownership – having common legal effects (the rights and obligations of an owner), but such a unification makes sense on the basis of the assumption that such legal effects share the same justification (enabling exclusive utilisation of goods and their voluntary transferral, without imposing negative externalities on third parties, etc.). Consequently, those who believe that no such common justification can be provided for all cases covered by the traditional concept of ownership tend to split the concept of ownership into different notions (distinguishing for example entitlements over

---

[28] Susan Haack, *Defending Science within Reason* (Amherst, New York 2003) 132. On 'generals', see Charles S. Peirce, 'The Cathegories', in: Susan Haack (ed.), *Pragmatism, old and new* (Amherst, New York 2006) 177–208.

[29] Lars Lindahl, 'Deduction and Justification in the Law. The Role of Legal Terms and Concepts', in: *Ratio Juris* 17 (2004), 182–201.

productive goods and entitlements over goods destined to private consumption). Similarly, it would make little sense to unify under a special concept all different offences punished with a particular sentence (for instance, all offences punished with a fine of 50 Euros).

8 Concepts in Legal Comparison and in Legal Doctrine

The distinction between possessing legal concepts and believing in their applicability is particularly significant for comparatist lawyers. As a comparatist lawyer, I may want to characterise a legal concept in inferential terms, but this characterisation should not automatically commit me to the belief that the corresponding inferential links hold in all legal systems: such links will hold only in those contexts where the concept is applicable, namely, where such inferences actually hold. My understanding of a concept does not commit me to any existential thesis, but is rather a heuristic tool that leads me to look for certain inferential links: my grasping the concept of patriarchal marriage leads me to search for certain inferential links (those constituting this concept), and to label the combination of such links accordingly, namely, as an implementation of the concept of patriarchal marriage (if I ever happen to find such a combination, either in the legal reality or in wrong legal beliefs).

Note, however, that the doctrinal commitment characterising the application of a concept (as opposed to the mere possession of that concept) can be undertaken implicitly, as when one provides an inferential characterisation of a term already used in one's linguistic community for describing a certain domain. In this case, unless I indicate that I am proposing an abstract characterisation of a concept (a characterisation looking for an application, rather than committed to particular applications), my specification of the inferential connections proper to that term will be understood as pre-supposing the existence of the category corresponding to my concept: such a specification will be understood as stating inferential connections that (I believe) really obtain in the domain at issue.[30] This is the case, for instance, when a lawyer is attributing certain inferential connections to a category of his or her legal system, using a term that is already in use within that system.

For instance, if I said without qualifications, in a discussion with Italian lawyers, that marriage entails the husband's power over the wife, I would not be understood as characterising a particular concept of marriage (like the notion of patriarchal marriage), which may not apply to the Italian context, but rather as stating what consequences are entailed by marriage according to Italian law (taking for granted

[30] By saying 'inferential connections that really obtain' I am not committing to a particular theory of legal reality. In fact, the distinction I am proposing (the distinction between possessing a concept and endorsing it), is compatible with all of the following views: that the existence of a legal inferential link is an empirically ascertainable fact, that it is a socio-institutional fact, or that it is a normative fact, consisting in normative justifiability.

that the marriage I am considering is indeed that situation that results from a marriage ceremony according to Italian law). Thus I would not only possess, in the sense of grasping or understanding, a particular concept of marriage (together with other concepts of marriage, each applicable to different real or hypothetical contexts), but I would (wrongly) assume that the category denoted by the concept of patriarchal marriage (that kind of relationship between husband and wife) exists in Italian law so that the ensuing normative qualifications (the husband's power and the wife's subjection) hold according to that law.

An existential assumption is usually presupposed when the doctrinal characterisations of a legal concept is tied to a certain legal system, so that the concept is assumed to apply to that legal system (the concept's inferential links are assumed to obtain in that system). In fact, a doctrinal characterisation of the concept expressed by a certain term is usually assumed to provide the correct meaning of the occurrences of the corresponding term in the legal sources. For instance, by characterising in a certain way the concept of self-defence or of property, I will be indicating how the occurrences of the term *self-defence* or *property* in authoritative texts are to be understood. Thus such a characterisation is supposed to provide inferential links (conditional norms) established by valid legal sources, inferential links that consequently hold in the considered legal systems determining the existence of a corresponding legal category. On the contrary comparative legal research and legal theory are not tied to a particular legal system: thus in these domains we need to distinguish the characterisation of a concept and the assumption that the concept applies to a certain domain (an assumption entailing that the concept's constitutive inferences obtain in that domain).

9 Conclusion

I hope to have convinced the reader that it is possible to understand the meaning of inferential legal concepts without undertaking any doctrinal commitment: we can consistently affirm that a legal concept is constituted by certain inferences while denying that such inferences obtain in the legal system we are considering, and consequently rejecting the conclusions derivable from the application of such inferences to known facts.

However, if we want to provide a doctrinally uncommitted inferential analysis of a legal concepts we must make it clear that we are just identifying an inferential pattern, possibly in order to model (wrong) opinions on the existing law, without implying that this pattern is part of the law. Usually the opposite will be presumed in doctrinal discourse. When we are engaged in such a discourse, our attempt at characterising a concept will usually be taken as the statement of inferences (norms) we believe to hold in the considered legal system. In other words, we will appear to make the assumption (of the existence of a category satisfying our inferences) made explicit by Ramsey and Carnap's analyses.

Acknowledgments Supported by the EU projects ONE-LEX (Marie Curie Chair), ESTRELLA (IST-2004-027665), and ALIS (IST- 2004-027968). Many thanks to Anna Pintore, Giorgio Volpe, and to the participants in the IVR-2007 Workshop on general legal concepts for their comments, suggestions and observations.

The Meaning of Legal Status Words

Jaap Hage

1 By Way of an Introduction

The law knows a number of words that stand for a particular status to which legal consequences are attached, but which has, apart from these legal consequences, no clear standing. These words include – for Dutch law – 'right holder', 'owner', 'mayor', and 'criminal suspect'. They differ – again for Dutch law – from other words such as 'obligation', which stands for a combination of a legal duty and a corresponding claim right, and 'sanction' which stands for a punishment or protective measure imposed by a judicial verdict.[1] The difference between legal status words and these last words is that in the latter case it is possible to specify their denotation by means of their application conditions, while that is not possible in case of legal status words. A criminal suspect *is* not a person against whom a reasonable suspicion exists of being an offender, or against whom criminal prosecution has been opened. Being a criminal suspect is rather a status which arises or perishes on particular grounds, to which a number of legal consequences are attached, and about which from a legal perspective not very much more can be said.

In Dutch law the status of criminal suspect is governed by article 27 of the Code of Criminal Procedure (Wetboek van Strafvordering). If somebody is a suspect, he is liable to have particular criminal proceedings executed against him. Article 27 specifies two different ways in which a person can be a criminal suspect, namely if there exists a reasonable suspicion that he is an offender, and if he is the object of criminal prosecution. However, being reasonably suspected of being an offender, and being the object of criminal prosecution are not two varieties on the stereotype of a suspect, but rather two disjoint ways of being a criminal suspect. So it would seem at first sight that the expression 'criminal suspect' is ambiguous and stands for two different things. However, if this were really the case, it would make sense to ask which different legal consequences are attached to each of these ways of

J. Hage (✉)
University of Maastricht, Maastricht, Netherlands
e-mail: jaap.hage@maastrichtuniversity.nl

[1] According to the 'Wet overdracht tenuitvoerlegging strafvonnisen'.

J.C. Hage, D. von der Pfordten (eds.), *Concepts in Law*, Law and Philosophy Library 88,
DOI 10.1007/978-90-481-2982-9_4, © Springer Science+Business Media B.V. 2009

being a suspect. In Dutch law, this question does not make sense, however, because both ways of being a suspect deal with the same legal status and therefore lead in principle to the same legal consequences. So, apparently, there is one status, which can be achieved in disjoint ways. This is characteristic for legal status words as they are discussed in this paper.

Because the nature of legal status is on beforehand not obvious, it seems interesting to elucidate this nature by analysing the meaning of legal status words. In this article I will try to answer the question after the meaning of legal status words, but before doing so I will say a little about the legal relevance of this question. Lawyer's interests in semantic issues often stem from the desire to determine the scope of application of legal rules. For instance, if there are rules concerning the amount of rent that can be asked for housing, lawyers want to know what counts as 'housing' to determine in which cases the rules are applicable. They may translate this question into the question what the word 'housing' means in the rules at issue, because this meaning is taken to determine the scope of application of the rules concerning the amount of rent.

Although it is quite customary among lawyers to address the question after the scope of application of a rule as one concerning the meaning of the words used in the rule formulation, this common practice should raise some doubts. To see why, we must first distinguish between on the one hand categories of things in the world, and on the other hand the words used to designate these categories. For instance, we have on the one hand the phenomenon (category) housing, and it is possible to raise questions about the proper demarcation of this phenomenon. What can still count as housing and what falls outside the boundaries of this category? This is, in philosophical terminology, an ontological question. It concerns the categories which exist in the world and their proper demarcation.

Philosophers have seriously disagreed over the issue whether categories exist independent of their instantiations. This issue about the ontological status of categories need not bother us here, and I only mention it to mark it off from the issue that should bother us, namely the demarcation of categories.[2] The point that I want to make here is that the demarcation of categories is an issue that belongs to the structure of reality, or maybe the operation of the human mind (if categorisation is approached from the perspective of cognitive psychology),[3] and is not primarily a matter of word meaning. What counts as an oak or as housing is not primarily a matter of what the words 'oak' and 'housing' mean. It is therefore somewhat surprising that lawyers nevertheless often treat it as a matter of word meaning.

---

[2] To some extent, the ontological status of categories is relevant. If categories are mind-independent (realism), the question whether something belongs to a category has an objective in the sense of mind-independent answer: something is objectively an oak, or a case of housing. It may be argued that some categories, for instance natural kinds, exist independent of human categorisation, while other categories are mind dependent. See the papers in S.S. Schwartz (ed.), *Naming, Necessity and Natural Kinds* (Ithaca 1977).

[3] See, for instance, the article 'Concepts and Induction' by E.E. Smith, in: M.I. Posner, *Foundations of Cognitive Science* (Cambridge 1991) 501–526.

The practical use of semantic questions in the law seems to be at first sight to establish the scope of application of legal rules, but at closer inspection this function of semantic questions turns out to be only marginally important. This holds to an even larger extent for legal status words, because of the doubts which exist whether their meanings can be identified with their application conditions. If one wants to determine whether a rule about owners is applicable in a particular case, knowledge of the meaning of 'owner' seems to be a dubitable asset. It seems more important to know how one becomes an owner or loses ownership than to know what 'owner' means. Therefore one should not expect from a general theory about the meaning of legal status words that it helps determine whether a rule applies to a particular case. However, one can expect from such a theory that it helps determine which knots must be cut if there is doubt about the applicability of a legal status word in a hard case.

Another, and even more important, use of a theory about the meaning of legal status words is that it contributes to our insight into the structure of legal systems. Indeed, the law consists to a large extent of relations between categories, in the form of definitions and rules that specify when particular words that refer to these categories apply. These relations are ultimately of crucial importance for the scope of application of mandatory rules. If we want to know how the law operates and coheres, we must know about these relations. Having a theory about the meaning of legal status words is a substantive part of this knowledge.

2 Tû-tû

In a paper going by the mysteriously sounding name of Tû-tû[4], the Danish legal philosopher Alf Ross addressed the question what the meaning is of words like 'ownership'. In this connection he drew a parallel with the use of the word tû-tû by the South Pacific Noît-cif tribe. If a member of that tribe did something wrong, such as killing a totem animal, or eating from the chief's food, he would become 'tû-tû'. As a consequence, this person was excluded from tribal ceremonies, and had to be subjected to a purification ceremony to take the 'tû-tû' state away. According to Ross, this state of being tû-tû does not really exist, and the word 'tû-tû' is meaningless. It only functions as a kind of placeholder between the different ways in which a person may become tû-tû and the consequences that are attached to being in this state.

Ross used this imaginary anthropological example to make a point about the meanings of legal terms, like 'right', 'duty' and 'owner'. In his opinion, these words are just as meaningless as the word 'tû-tû', and their role is confined to that of intermediary in legal argument chains. Let us take the word 'owner' as an example. The law knows several ways to obtain ownership, such as creation of a good, inheritance, or transfer of the right. Moreover, the law attaches many legal consequences

---

[4] A. Ross. 'Tû-Tû' 70 *Harvard Law Review* (1957), 812–825.

to being an owner, such as the duty for everybody except the owner not to destroy the owned good, and the competence of the owner to transfer the ownership, or to create a more limited right (e.g. mortgage) with respect to the owned object.

In theory, the legal consequences of being an owner might be attached directly to all the different ways in which ownership can be acquired. For instance, one might have the rule that if one has inherited a good, all other persons have the duty not to destroy this good. In this way it is possible to do without ownership altogether, because all the legal consequences that are traditionally attached to the existence of this right are then attached to all different ways of what would traditionally be ways of acquiring ownership. If there are three ways to become owner of a good, and if there are four legal consequences attached to ownership, twelve rules are required to bring about the necessary connections (see Fig. 1).

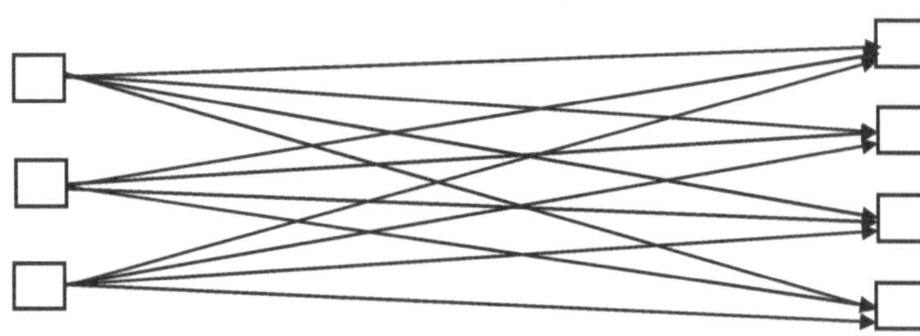

Fig. 1

It is more economical, however, to work with an intermediate category – the category of ownership – that forms the intermediary between the rules that specify under which circumstances particular legal consequences obtain, and the rules that specify which legal consequences obtain if the conditions of the former rules are satisfied. If there are three ways to acquire ownership and four legal consequences are attached to ownership, a legal system that uses the category of ownership, needs seven rules to regulate this subject (see Fig. 2).

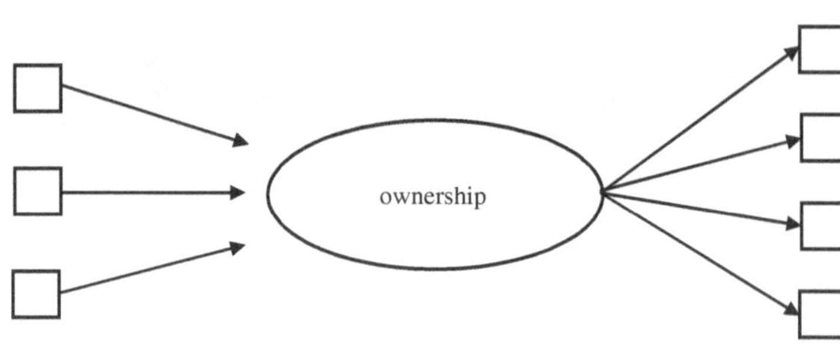

Fig. 2

According to Alf Ross, legal status words such as 'right' and 'ownership' lack semantic reference, just as the word tû-tû. Their meanings are empty; they are nothing more than intermediaries in arguments from the conditions that specify when these words are applicable to the consequences of their applicability.

In this paper I will address two questions. The first one is whether legal status words have semantic reference. I will argue that the answer to this question should be affirmative: legal status words have meanings in the sense of semantic reference. The argument for this thesis requires a discussion about the nature of social reality and the place of the law within this social reality. In this discussion I will take side with the so-called 'institutional approach' to the law.[5]

The second question is whether a tû-tû style, or inferential, analysis can help to specify the meanings of legal status words. The answer to this second question will be shaded. On the one hand, an inferential analysis cannot give the *meanings* of legal status words, or – as a matter of fact – of any words. On the other hand, the availability of an inferential analysis is a big step towards *understanding the meaning* of a legal status word. The distinction between the meaning of words and understanding their meaning is in my opinion crucial for the evaluation of the role of semantics in legal theory.

3 Social, Institutional and Legal Facts

Ross' view that legal status words lack semantic reference is hardly substantiated in his paper. The only arguments Ross presents for his position are a reference to work of Lundstedt[6] who shares Ross' opinion, and a parallel with the use of the word tû-tû, which he assumes to be meaningless. It may be granted that words like 'right', 'duty', and 'ownership' lack physical reference, but, as I will briefly argue, legal status words refer to institutional entities, which are a subspecies of social entities which exist in social reality.

The first step in this argument is to distinguish between physical reality, which is usually taken to exist independently of what people think about it,[7] and social reality. Next to the presumably mind-independent physical reality there exists also a social reality. There are facts that belong to this social reality, such as the fact that money

---

[5] This approach is described in, amongst others, N. MacCormick and O. Weinberger, *An Institutional Theory of Law* (Dordrecht 1986), E. Lagerspetz, *The Opposite Mirrors* (Dordrecht 1995), M. la Torre, *Norme, Instituzioni, Valore: per una teoria instituzionalistica del diritto* (Rome 1999), D.W.P. Ruiter, *Institutional Legal Facts* and *Legal Institutions* (Dordrecht 1993 and 2001), and N. MacCormick, *Institutions of Law* (Oxford 2007).

[6] A.V. Lundstedt, *Die Unwissenschaftlichkeit der Rechtswissenschaft. Band. I: Die falschen Vorstellungen von objektivem Recht und subjektiven Rechten* (Berlin 1932).

[7] In general, the assumption that physical reality exists independent of human perception or what humans think or believe about it, marks off ontological realists from ontological idealists. See M. Devitt, *Realism and Truth*, 2nd edition (Oxford 1991) 13–16, and J.R. Searle, *The construction of social reality* (New York 1995) 149–155.

Since my own ontological views tend towards some form of idealism (see J.C. Hage, *Studies in Legal Logic* (Dordrecht 2005) 176–184), I write about the mind-independence of the physical world *as if* I adopted realism for this part of reality.

can be used to make payments, the fact that there is animosity between the pupils of two neighbouring schools, or the fact that the chairman of the university department makes a lot of effort to increase the ties between the members of his department. In these facts figure some entities which only exist in social reality. Money is an example of such an entity, just as animosity and a university department.

Social facts can obtain in at least two ways. One way is that sufficiently many members of a social group believe that these facts obtain because they are believed to obtain, and also believe that most of the other members believe the same, namely that these facts obtain because they are believed to obtain and that the other members believe the same.[8] For instance, there exists animosity between the pupils of two schools if most of these pupils experience and believe there is animosity and that the other pupils experience and believe the same. I will call facts that exist in social reality because they are believed or experienced by most (relevant) members of a social group *basic social facts*.

The other way in which a fact can exist in social reality is as an *institutional fact*. A fact exists as an institutional fact if (and only if) there exists a rule in social reality that attaches the existence of this fact to the existence of other facts.[9] These other facts may, but need not, be social facts themselves. For instance the fact that John is punishable is an institutional fact. It is attached to the fact that John is a thief by the rule that makes thieves punishable. Another example would be the existence of money and the possibility to use money for making payments. The existence of money and its use is presently regulated by the law, which is a phenomenon that exists in social reality itself.

A fact can both exist as a basic and as an institutional social fact. It is even so that social facts that exist as institutional facts will normally also be basic social facts. If this is not the case, that is if an institutional fact is broadly not recognised, the question whether this fact obtains has no easy answer.[10] For the rest of this paper I will ignore the concurrence between basic and institutional social facts, because it is not directly relevant for the issue at stake, namely the meaning of legal status words.

It is possible to mark off the part of social reality that exists because of rules as *institutional reality*. The law and the facts that belong to it are part of social reality and most – but not all – of the law belongs to institutional reality. The part of social reality that specifically belongs to the law consists of what I will call *legal facts* and

---

[8] In general there exists an extensive literature on the existence of social reality, which cannot be explored here. The present brief discussion should suffice to establish that legal status words have semantic reference.

[9] This theme is explored in N. MacCormick, 'Law as Institutional Fact', in MacCormick and Weinberger, *An Institutional Theory of Law*, 49–76.

[10] A well-known example of such a situation from the law is that a statutory rule is broadly not recognised as valid, for instance because it is experienced as unjust. This rule is valid to the extent that it was validly made, and invalid because it is broadly not recognised as a valid legal rule. One aspect or interpretation of the discussion between legal positivists and natural law theorists seems to hinge on this discrepancy.

legal entities. Organisations like the United Nations and the Strasbourg Court for Human Rights, for instance, are legal entities which thank their existence to treaty provisions by means of which they were instituted.

Both the existence and the consequences of legal facts are regulated by legal rules.[11] I will use the legal fact that Jones owns the farm Blackacre as an example. There are rules that specify under which circumstances somebody becomes the owner of a piece of real property. For instance, Jones may have inherited Blackacre from his mother and has thus become the owner. This is made possible by a rule of law stating that one can become the owner of real property through inheritance. Obviously there are more rules that specify how to become an owner, and these rules make it possible to become the owner (of real property) in many different ways. Let us call the rules specifying how some legal status, such as ownership, is obtained the *entrance rules* for this status.

There are also many rules that specify how ownership is lost. For instance, Jones will lose his ownership if he transfers it to a railway company, or if he passes away. If ownership resides in chattel, it may also end because the object of ownership, for instance a car, is destroyed. Let us call the rules specifying how some legal status is lost the *exit rules* of this status.

Finally there are rules that attach legal consequences to ownership. For instance, the owner of real property will be able to take legal measures against trespassers, have the competence to mortgage his property, or to transfer it. Moreover, the owner may have the duty to make access to his land safe for innocent by-passers and have to pay the taxes attached to the ownership of real property. Let us call the rules specifying the legal consequences of some legal status the *consequential rules* of this status.

Notice that the consequential rules of one status may function as entrance rules for another status. For instance, the tax law of a country may use the status of 'real estate owner'. A real estate owner has special duties with regard to bookkeeping and making tax declarations. If somebody becomes the owner (a legal status) of a piece of real estate, she thereby automatically (because of a consequential rule of being an owner) becomes a real estate owner in the sense of tax law. When she loses the ownership, she also loses the status of real estate owner. (see Fig. 3.)

The entrance, exit and consequential rules connected to some legal status such as ownership together specify what, from the legal point of view, is relevant in connection with this status. In the following sections I will address the issue what the relevance of these rules is for the meaning of legal status words. More in particular I will discuss by way of example to what extent the meaning of 'ownership' or the verb 'owns' is governed by the entrance, exit and consequential rules for ownership.

---

[11] Because the law is not completely institutionalised, this regulation is not exhaustive. This means that there can be legal facts which only obtain as basic social facts, and not as institutional legal facts. For the purposes of the present paper, however, the institutional legal facts are the most relevant.

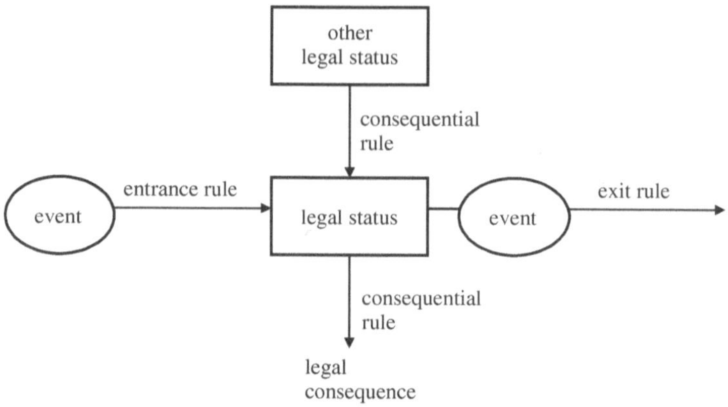

Fig. 3

4 Criteria Theories of Meaning

In connection with 'descriptive' words such as 'table', 'love', 'runs' and 'owns' it is customary to distinguish between their extensions (tables, cases of love, running persons or animals, and pairs of owners and what is owned) and their intensions, the criteria for their application, or – which is not necessarily the same – the means by which the members of the extension are identified.[12] Depending on whether primacy is attributed to the intension or the extension of the word, one can distinguish between respectively criteria theories of meaning and theories of direct reference.

The most familiar form of a criteria theory of meaning is the theory that the meaning of a sentence is given by its truth conditions, and that the meanings of descriptive words are given with their conditions of applicability.[13] In this connection it is possible to distinguish between sober and componential conditions. Sober conditions use the words of which the meaning is specified in the specification of their meanings. Examples are 'The sentence "It is raining" means that (is true if and only if) it is raining' and 'The word "dog" stands for (is applicable to) dogs'.[14] Sober analyses have the advantage that they give the exact meanings of words and sentences. Their obvious disadvantage is that they are of little use to somebody who does not know the meaning of the word or sentence at issue, and that they give no indication how meaning helps the speaker of a language use words and sentences correctly.

---

[12] See, for instance, T. Crane, 'Meaning', in T. Honderich (ed.), *The Oxford Companion to Philosophy* (Oxford 1995) 541–542 and B. Hale and C. Wright (eds.), *A Companion to the Philosophy of Language* (Oxford 1997) 663–664.

[13] Cf. D. Wiggins, 'Meaning and truth conditions: from Frege's grand design to Davidson's', in Hale and Wright (eds.), *A Companion to the Philosophy of Language*, 3–28.

[14] The program of sober analyses has become associated with the work of Donald Davidson, starting with his paper 'Truth and Meaning' in D. Davidson, *Inquiries into Truth and Interpretation* (Oxford 1984) 17–36.

In a componential analysis of meaning, there are usually several conditions which do not use the words of which the meanings are specified. Examples would be 'The sentence "It is raining" means that (is true if and only if) there are drops of water falling down from the sky, caused by condensation in the clouds', and 'The word "dog" stands for (is applicable to) four-legged domesticated animals that bark'. Associated with componential analyses is the idea of meaning rules. These rules, which govern the meanings of words and, indirectly, of sentences, specify the criteria for the use of words and the truth conditions of sentences. A componential analysis of meaning has the advantage that it is useful to instruct the meanings of words and sentences and to make understandable how somebody who knows the meaning of a word or sentence, is capable to use this word or sentence correctly.

An important thing to notice about componential analyses is that they make word meanings perform two functions at the same time. On the one hand these meanings bring about a coupling between a word and the 'things' denoted by it, and on the other hand they demarcate the boundaries of this category of things. In schema (Fig. 4):

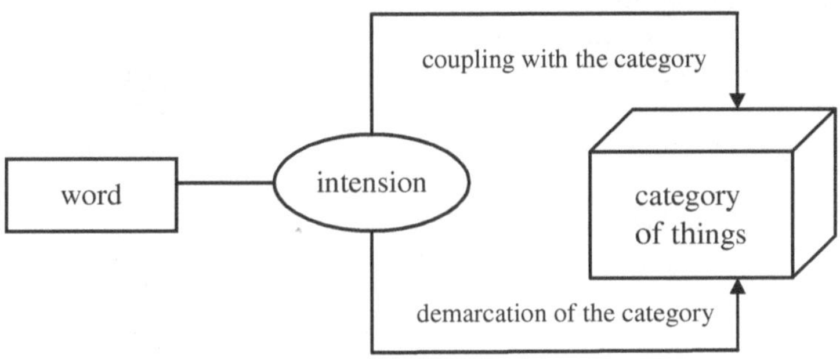

Fig. 4

The above examples of componential analyses of meaning may not be convincing. Although this may be caused by a lack of imagination of the author, I take it that something more serious is at stake. In my opinion, a componential analysis only makes sense in case of words and sentences with artificially assigned meanings, based on stipulative definitions, such as 'laser' or – in the legal sphere – 'obligation'. Although a speaker of a language normally can recognise instances of a word's denotation, he does not know precise criteria by means of which these instances can be identified, let alone that he knows the precise criteria that give the word's meaning. Most people know how to recognise normal dogs under normal circumstances, but they do not know any criteria specifying the meaning of the word 'dog' and not even criteria by means of which they usually recognise dogs.[15] Apparently it is possible to know the meaning of a word or sentence without

[15] This issue is discussed more extensively in J.C. Hage, *Feiten en betekenis* (Facts and meaning), Ph.D.-thesis, Leiden 1987, Chapter IV (in Dutch).

knowing the componential conditions of applicability of the word, or the sentences componential truth conditions, which goes to show that these meanings cannot be identified with componential criteria. The view that there are meaning rules specifying the conditions for the correct use of descriptive words appears therefore to be wrong.

5 Theories of Direct Reference

Theories of direct reference were primarily developed to account for the way in which proper names[16] and definite descriptions[17] are used to refer to individuals and how descriptive words denote natural kinds.[18] They can, however, also be used to account for the meanings of descriptive words that do not denote natural kinds, such as 'computer', 'car', and 'mountain'. The general idea behind this use is that such words directly, that is without an intermediate role for intensions, denote a kind of entities and that their meanings are given with this denotation. This means that word meaning only performs one of the two functions mentioned before; it only couples the word with the category of things, without also delineating this category. Although a speaker may associate certain characteristics with such a words, and use these characteristics to identify instances of the word's denotation, these characteristics are not an intension that delineates the category and in that sense contributes to the 'meaning' of the word. So, for instance, the meaning of the word 'dog' is that it refers to dogs, and that is all that is to be said about the meaning of this word. In particular the meaning of 'dog' does not determine what dogs are.

Although intensions play no role in direct reference theories of meaning, this does not mean that associated characteristics have no role at all in connection with word meaning. Somebody who knows that the word 'dog' stands for dogs, but is not able to use the word correctly in the presence or absence of dogs (saying that there is no dog when there is one, and vice versa) does not know the meaning of 'dog' properly. To state it differently, it is not well possible to know what 'dog' means without knowing at least to some extent what dogs are. More generally, knowing the meaning of a descriptive word according to a direct reference theory of meaning involves having some knowledge about the word's denotation. So, although the meaning of a descriptive word is exhaustively given by the word's denotation, without intervening role of associated characteristics in the form of an intention, *knowledge* of the meaning requires some knowledge of these associated

---

[16] S.A. Kripke. 'Naming and necessity', in D. Davidson and G. Harman (eds.), *Semantics of natural language*, 2nd edition (Dordrecht 1972) 253–355.

[17] K.S. Donnellan. 'Reference and Definite Descriptions' LXXV *The Philosophical Review* (1966), 281–304.

[18] H.Putnam, 'The Meaning of 'Meaning' ' in H. Putnam, *Mind, Language and Reality; Philosophical Papers, vol. 2* (Cambridge, Mass. 1975) 215–271.

characteristics, because knowledge of a word's meaning involves knowledge about the word's denotation.[19]

This is still quite vague, because there may be much to know about a word's denotation, and it is unclear which part of this knowledge is necessary to know the meaning of the word. For instance, what should one know about dogs in order to know what 'dog' means? Presumably sufficient to recognise normal dogs under normal circumstances, but as this repeated use of the word 'normal' indicates, even this standard leaves much to be specified. Different people may use different techniques to recognise dogs. Blind people, for instance, cannot use the visual appearance of dogs as means to identify them, while deaf people cannot hear dogs barking. This is problematic for a componential analysis of meaning, because the latter kind of theory would be committed to the existence of an unique answer to the question which technique of recognizing dogs would coincide with the meaning of 'dog'. In a direct reference theory of meaning, however, the existence of one meaning (that is: denotation) can go together with the existence of different techniques for identifying members of this denotation. So even if different people have completely different techniques of identifying the members of a word's denotation, this is well compatible with this word's having an unique meaning in the form of the relation to its denotation. The different techniques merely represent different ways to recognise the items for which the word stands. Presumably the question what one needs to know about a word's denotation in order to know the word's meaning does not have a precise answer.

6 The Meaning of 'Owns'

If one expects from the meaning of a word that it provides us with the conditions for this word's applicability, the meaning of the legal status word 'owns' or 'ownership' is given with the entry rules for this status, or – to state it in ordinary language – by the rules that tell us how ownership can be obtained. It seems, however, strange to identify the ways in which one can become owner with the meaning of 'owns' or 'ownership'. Apparently a sober analysis is more in place; 'ownership' stands for ownership, and 'owns' stands for a relation between a person and some object (in a broad sense) namely that this persons owns that object. The answer to the question whether inferential analysis can help to specify the meanings of legal status words in general and the meaning of the word 'owns' in particular is in this sense negative.

---

[19] By making this distinction between a word's meaning and knowing what a word means, I deviate from Michael Dummett's ideas about the meaning of words, According to the 'full-blooded' theories advocated by Dummett, theories of meaning should specify what is necessary to know how to apply a word. On this view, what I call 'meaning' and 'knowledge of meaning' are both incorporated in a full-blooded theory of meaning. See M. Dummett, 'What is a Theory of meaning (I)', in M. Dummett, *The Seas of Language* (Oxford 1993) 1–33. J. Skorupsi, 'Meaning, use, verification', in Hale and Wright (eds.), *A Companion to the Philosophy of Language*, 29–59, provides background information about these so-called 'verificationist theories of meaning'.

An inferential analysis can, however, be useful to specify those characteristics of ownership that need to be known by somebody who *knows what ownership involves*.

The rules that deal with ownership, entry rules, exit rules and consequential rules, are rules of positive law. In theory, every legal system may have different rules concerning ownership and in practice two legal systems will seldom or never have exactly the same sets of entry, exit and consequential rules about ownership. In this sense, ownership involves one thing in one legal system, and another thing in another legal system. However, if some legal system had the rule that one can acquire ownership of a thing by punching the present owner on the nose, that one loses ownership of everything one owns if one is punched on the nose, or if one wins the national lottery, and that the only consequence of owning something is that one has to mention this fact everyday to one's mother, we would probably say that the word 'owns' in this system is used for something different than what we use it for.

To state it more generally, although the rules that deal with ownership may vary from one legal system to another, the differences between different systems may not be too large, or too important, because otherwise the word 'owns' stands for different things in different systems. In this respect, the different versions of ownership can be compared to different species that belong to one genus. Just as one can raise the question how different horses can be in order to count still as horses, one can ask how different several versions of ownership can be in order to count still as different versions of the same legal institution. The important point in connection with the subject of this paper is that the relevant characteristics of the different versions of ownership are too a large extent given with the entry, consequential and exit rules connected to this institution.[20]

7 Conclusion

The meanings of legal status words are that they stand for specific legal statuses and nothing else. These statuses are not non-existent, as Alf Ross suggested; they are real phenomena in (the institutionalised part of) social reality.

An inferential analysis that is concerned with the entry, consequential and exit rules for a legal status is important for understanding the nature of the thus analysed legal status. Some degree of such an understanding is necessary to know what a status is, and therefore also for *knowing* the meaning of the corresponding status word. An inferential analysis does not provide us with the meaning of a legal status word, however.

[20] Arguably there are other factors relevant for the way in which ownership functions in a society. It may, for instance, be very important whether means of production are privately owned, and whether the owners of real property have important political functions in a society. It may seem that these factors do not determine what ownership *is*, but how ownership *functions* in a society. Whether this distinction between what something is, and how it functions is a sharp one may, however, be doubted.

Explicating the Concept of Legal Competence

Torben Spaak

1 Introduction

In everyday language the term 'competence' can mean *proficiency* or *authority*. A person can be a competent decision maker in the sense that as a rule he makes good and right decisions, but he can also be competent in the sense that he has the authority to make certain kinds of decision. My concern here is with competence in the sense of authority.[1] The concept of legal competence, thus conceived, is a normative concept, in the sense that a person has competence by virtue of a norm, and that the exercise of competence changes a person's normative position.

In this article, I argue (i) that we need a concept of legal competence to be able to discuss questions of legal validity and invalidity in a clear and fruitful way. I also defend an explication of the competence concept, according to which (ii) a person, *p*, *has* the competence in regard to a legal position, *LP*, if, and only if, there is an action, *a*, and a situation, *S*, such that if *p* in *S* performs *a*, and thus goes about it in the right way, *p* will, through *a*, change *LP*; and (iii) *p exercises* his competence by performing a special type of act, which is such that it depends for its legal effect on having been performed with the (actual or imputed) intent to bring about the said effect. In addition, I argue (iv) that we should distinguish (a) between autonomous and heteronomous competence, and (b) between norm-creating and regulative competence.

I begin with a few words about concepts and the explication of concepts in general (Sections 2 and 3). I then turn to consider the concept of legal competence, beginning with a look at what some distinguished legal scholars have said about this concept (Section 4), and proceeding to consider a difficulty in their (and mine) understanding of the concept that arises when the concept is applied to the

T. Spaak (✉)
Department of Law, Uppsala University, Uppsala, Sweden
e-mail: Torben.Spaak@jur.uu.se

[1] I use, as the reader will have noticed, the term 'legal competence' and not the term 'legal power' to designate the concept in question, and in doing so I follow what might be called a Scandinavian, perhaps even a European, tradition within the philosophy of law. See Lars Lindahl, *Position and Change* (Dordrecht 1977) 194.

J.C. Hage, D. von der Pfordten (eds.), *Concepts in Law*, Law and Philosophy Library 88,
DOI 10.1007/978-90-481-2982-9_5, © Springer Science+Business Media B.V. 2009

separation of powers doctrine (Section 5). Having done that, I make a distinction between having and exercising legal competence (Sections 6 and 7) and between some different types of legal competence (Section 8). I conclude the article with a brief discussion of the adequacy of the proposed explication (Section 9).

2 Concepts

There is little agreement about the nature of concepts. Some conceive of concepts as psychological entities, viz. mental representations, others conceive of them as abilities, and yet others conceive of them as meanings, specifically Fregean senses.[2] I shall assume in what follows that a concept is the meaning of a word or an expression, specifically its Fregean sense.[3] On this analysis, a word or an expression, say, 'right' may express the same concept as another word or expression in the same or in a different language. And if a word or expression is ambiguous, if it has more than one meaning, then it simply expresses more than one concept. Moreover, on this analysis the meaning or *intension* of a word or an expression determines its *extension*, that is, the class of (abstract or concrete) objects to which the word applies. Of course, this analysis does not apply to so-called natural kind words, such as 'water,' 'gold,' 'tiger,' etc., since these (are said to) have meaning by virtue of being causally related to the corresponding natural kind (water, gold, tiger, etc.).[4] Luckily, natural kind words play little role in legal thinking,[5] and legal competence is in any case not a natural kind.[6]

---

[2] For more on this topic, see Eric Margolis and Stephen Laurence, 'Concepts,' in: Edward N. Zalta (ed.), *The Stanford Encyclopedia of Philosophy (Spring 2006 Edition)*, URL = <http://plato.stanford.edu/archives/spr2006/entries/concepts/>. As is well known, Frege distinguished between the sense and the reference of a word. Gottlob Frege, 'On Sense and Meaning,' in: Peter Geach and Max Black (eds.), *Translations from the Philosophical Writings of Gottlob Frege*. 3rd edition (Totowa 1980) 56–78. He did not, however, think of concepts as the sense of a word, but as its *reference*. Thus, on Frege's analysis a predicate such as 'is wise' refers to, but does not express, a concept. Gottlob Frege, 'On Concept and Object,' in: Geach and Black, *Translations*, 42–55.

[3] Joseph Raz maintains that it is a mistake to identify concepts with the meanings of words, suggesting instead that, metaphorically speaking, 'concepts... are placed between the world, aspects of which they are concepts of, and words or phrases, which express them (the concepts) and are used to talk about those aspects of the world.' See Joseph Raz, 'Can There Be a Theory of Law?', in: Martin P. Golding and William A. Edmundson (eds.), *The Blackwell Guide to the Philosophy of Law and Legal Theory* (Oxford 2005) 324–242, 325. But if this doesn't mean that concepts are Fregean senses, what does it mean?

[4] For more about natural kinds and natural-kind words, see, e.g., Mark Platts, *Ways of Meaning*. 2nd edition (London and Cambridge 1997) Ch. XI. See also Michael Devitt and Kim Sterelny, *Language and Reality*, 2nd edition (Cambridge, Massachusetts 1999) Chs. 4–5; Michael S Moore, 'Law as a Functional Kind,' in: Michael S. Moore, *Educating Oneself in Public* (Oxford 2000) 294–332, 309–311.

[5] But see Michael S. Moore, 'A Natural Law Theory of Interpretation,' *Southern California Law Review* 58 (1985) 277–398; Nicos Stavropoulos, *Objectivity in Law* (Oxford 1996) Ch. 2.

[6] For an in-depth analysis and consequent rejection of the idea that natural-kinds analysis can successfully be applied to the concept of law, see Jules L Coleman and Ori Simchen, 'Law,' *Legal*

I believe this way of conceiving of concepts (as Fregean senses) is attractive, primarily because it seems to me to be more or less accurate, but also because it mirrors (what I take to be) our common sense understanding of concepts. True, like the other ways of conceiving of concepts mentioned above, it has its problems.[7] I do not, however, wish to argue that this way of conceiving of concepts is unproblematic, only that it is defensible.

3 Explication of Concepts

To explicate (or rationally reconstruct) a concept X, amounts to transforming X, which we may call the *explicandum*, into a concept that is more exact, which we may call the *explicatum*, while retaining its intuitive content, in order to make it more functional for a certain purpose – in this case, to be a concept that we can make use of to analyse and discuss questions of legal validity and invalidity. As Rudolf Carnap explains, an explication of a concept is adequate if, and only if, the *explicatum* is (i) similar to the *explicandum*, as well as (ii) exact, (iii) fruitful, and (iv) simple.[8] Clearly, an explication of a concept is partly prescriptive, and this means that a given explication will not be true or false, but rather useful or not useful for a certain purpose.

I think of my analysis of the concept of legal competence put forward in this article as an explication of the concept of legal competence described in the quotations from the writings of the four distinguished legal scholars introduced in Section 4 below. That is to say, I think of my analysis of the concept of legal competence as a refined version of the concept of legal competence described by these authors.

4 Legal Scholars on the Concept of Legal Competence

The competence concept can be sought out in at least two different ways: we may study the way legal practitioners make use of the concept in their argumentation, or we may study what legal scholars and philosophers have said about the concept. I believe the latter alternative is preferable, since it is rather unclear how legal practitioners conceive of the competence concept, if they make use of such a concept at all. To be sure, a judge or an attorney may say things like 'Since Smith was not authorised to act on behalf of Jones, Jones is not bound by the contract that Smith entered into with Brown,' or 'The District Court in Uppsala has no power to try this case'. But as far as I can tell, legal practitioners do not operate with a *general* concept of legal competence, such as the concept I am concerned with in this article; and if they do, after all, make use of such a concept, it is rather unclear

Theory 9 (2003) 1–41. See also Brian Bix, 'Can Theories of Meaning and Reference Solve the Problem of Legal Determinacy?', *Ratio Juris* 16:3 (2003) 281–295.

[7] See, e.g., Margolis and Laurence, *Concepts*, 4.

[8] Rudolf Carnap, *Logical Foundations of Probability*, 2nd edition (Chicago 1967) 5–7. See also Rudolf Carnap, *Meaning and Necessity*, 2nd edition (Chicago 1956) 7–8.

how they conceive of it. Let us therefore take a look at what some distinguished and, in my view, representative, legal scholars have said about the concept of legal competence.

Wesley Hohfeld distinguished eight legal concepts that he thought of as being fundamental in legal thinking. Among these was the concept of legal competence, or, as Hohfeld said, the concept of legal power:

> A change in a given legal relation may result (1) from some superadded fact or group of facts not under the volitional control of a human being (or human beings); or (2) from some superadded fact or group of facts which are under the volitional control of one or more human beings. As regards the second class of cases, the person (or persons) whose volitional control is paramount may be said to have the (legal) power to effect the particular change of legal relations that is involved in the problem.[9]

Hans Kelsen, too, analysed the concept of legal competence. The following statement illustrates his views on this concept:

> Die normative Funktion des Ermächtigens bedeutet: einem Individuum die Macht verleihen, Normen zu setzen und anzuwenden. Eine Moralnorm ermächtigt den Vater, seinem Kind verbindliche Befehle zu geben. Eine Rechtsnorm ermächtigt bestimmte Individuen Rechtsnormen zu erzeugen oder Rechtsnormen anzuwenden. In diesen Fällen sagt man: das Recht verleihe bestimmten Individuen eine Rechtsmacht... Ein nicht dazu ermächtigtes Individuum kann nicht Recht erzeugen oder Recht anwenden. Seine Akte haben objektiv nicht den Charakter von Rechtserzeugung oder Rechtsanwendung, auch wenn sie subjektiv in dieser Absicht erfolgen. Ihr subjektiver Sinn ist nicht ihr objektiver Sinn. Diese Akte haben – wie man sagt – keine Rechtswirkung, sie sind nichtig, d.h. rechtlich nicht vorhanden.[10]

Another legal philosopher who concerned himself with the concept of legal competence was Alf Ross, who stated the following about this concept:

> Competence is the legally established ability to create legal norms (or legal effects) through and in accordance with enunciations to this effect. Those enunciations in which competence is exercised are called actes juridiques, or acts-in-the-law, or in private law, dispositive declarations. Examples are: a promise, a will, a judgment, an administrative license, a statute. An act-in-the-law is, like a move in chess, a human act which nobody can perform as an exercise of his natural faculties.... Since a norm of competence prescribes the conditions for the creation of a norm it is a tautology to say that if an attempt is made to exercise competence *ultra vires* (outside the scope of the competence) no legal norm is created. This is expressed by saying that the intended act-in-the-law is invalid or that non-compliance with a norm of competence results in invalidity.[11]

H. L. A. Hart also took an interest in the concept of legal competence, or, as he said, the concept of legal power. Criticizing John Austin's command theory of law, he pointed out that it could not account for the existence of power-conferring rules,

---

[9] Wesley Newcomb Hohfeld, *Fundamental Legal Conceptions as Applied in Judicial Reasoning. With an Introduction by Nigel Simmonds*, edited by David Campbell and Philip Thomas (Dartmouth 2001) 21.

[10] Hans Kelsen, *Allgemeine Theorie der Normen*, edited by Kurt Ringhofer and Robert Walter (Wien 1979) 82.

[11] Alf Ross, *Directives and Norms* (London 1968) 130–131.

that is, rules that '... provide individuals with facilities for realizing their wishes, by conferring legal powers upon them to create, by certain specified procedures and subject to certain conditions, structures of rights and duties within the coercive framework of the law.'[12]

We see that these authors are generally in agreement about at least the following three points:

(1) *One who has competence has the possibility of changing legal positions.*[13] To be sure, one could say with several of the writers quoted above, that the competent person has an ability or a power to change legal positions. I choose, however, to say that he has the *possibility*, because I believe that the terms 'ability' and 'power', properly understood, primarily have to do with physical or mental qualities, while the term 'possibility' may well be used in normative as well as non-normative language.
(2) *Competence is a necessary condition for legal validity.* At least Kelsen, Hart and Ross seem to think that competence is a necessary condition for validity, but the same can probably be said of Hohfeld, too. In saying that the competent person has the possibility of changing legal positions, they indicate that to their minds a person can exercise his competence only by performing a valid act.
(3) *The agent changes legal positions by performing a special kind of act.* In the quotations above only Ross says explicitly that it is a question of a special kind of act, namely an act-in-the-law, but it seems that the other writers, too, believe that competence is exercised by the performance of a special kind of act. I will call this type of act a C-act (a competence-exercising act).

It should be emphasised, though, that the agent does not have competence in general terms, but only in a certain respect. For our purposes it is therefore convenient to conceive of the competence relation as a two-place relation: it is always a certain person who has competence in a certain respect. In this respect, the concept of competence resembles concepts like 'owner,' 'father,' and 'brother.' Thus a statement of the type

(1) p has competence

is elliptical and should be understood in the following way:

(1*) p has competence in regard to *LP*,

where *LP* is a legal position that can be described using Hohfeld's fundamental legal concepts.[14] This makes it possible to distinguish between those cases where the agent, by performing a C-act

---

[12] H.L.A. Hart, *The Concept of Law* (Oxford 1961) 27.
[13] I mean by a 'legal position' an n-place legal relation with $n \geq 1$. For more on the concept of a legal position, see Spaak, *The Concept of Legal Competence*, 76–79.
[14] See Hohfeld, *Fundamental Legal Conceptions*, 11–31.

(i) brings about the intended change of position,
(ii) brings about some other change of position, and
(iii) does not bring about any change of position at all.

When the agent, by performing a C-act, brings about the intended change of position, we say that he exercises his competence.

In light of the said, I propose the following tentative definition of the concept of legal competence:

(D.1) A person, *p*, has the competence in regard to a legal position, *LP*, if, and only if, there is a C-act, *a*, such that *p* has the possibility, by performing *a*, of changing *LP*.

The concept of competence thus conceived constitutes a lowest common denominator for the competence concepts of positive law, such as *Geschäftsfähigkeit*, *Prozessfähigkeit*, or *Kompetenz*.[15] The difference between the (general) concept of competence expressed in (D.1) and the competence concepts of positive law just mentioned is that the content of the latter are more specific in that they concern only, say, private law or the law of procedure.

5 A Difficulty: Competence and the Separation of Powers

I said above that we need a concept of legal competence in order to be able to analyse and discuss questions of legal validity and invalidity in a clear and fruitful way. The reason, of course, is that competence is a necessary condition for legal validity, in the sense that only a competent person can change legal positions – if you lack the competence, you cannot change legal positions, even if you perform the competence-exercising act properly and in accordance with any formal requirements laid down by the pertinent legal norms. Thus if the legislature makes an attempt to legislate in a field in which it lacks the competence to legislate, or in which its competence is in some way circumscribed, perhaps by a bill of rights, then the attempted piece of legislation will be null and void, or will at least be declared invalid by a court if attacked.

But a problem arises when one applies the competence concept to the separation of powers doctrine. As is well known, the separation of powers doctrine divides the competences of the government into three separate spheres, viz. legislative competence, executive competence, and judicial competence, and requires that the legislative, the executive, and the judicial branch operate within the sphere allotted to that particular branch, and only within that sphere. If, however, the separation of powers doctrine concerns the *competences* of the different branches, one expects that an

---

[15] As the reader will have noticed, I make use of German terms to express the concepts I have in mind. The reason is that the import of the corresponding concepts are reasonably clear to me: whereas these concepts are familiar to Swedish legal scholars, the more or less equivalent concepts found in common law jurisdictions are not. For more on this topic, see Spaak, *The Concept of Legal Competence*, 11–17.

attempt on the part of an organ in one branch to exercise competence that properly belongs to an organ in another branch will necessarily fail, in the sense that the intended change of legal positions will not occur. But this does not always seem to be the case.

Consider in this regard the problem about judicial law-making as it is presented in the so-called judicial activism/judicial restraint debate.[16] For the purposes of this discussion, we may rather crudely take activist judges to be willing not only to apply pre-existing law, but also to *create law* when doing so is likely to further social aims that they embrace[17], and judges who practice restraint to insist on sticking to the application of pre-existing law rather narrowly conceived, because and in so far as doing so means respecting decisions by the other branches of government.[18] We see that thus conceived the activism/restraint debate proceeds on the assumption that courts do have the competence to create law, and this indicates that the debate is really about the *permissibility* or the appropriateness, not the possibility, of judicial law-making.

What to do? Should we adjust the view that the separation of powers doctrine concerns the competences of the government, should we adjust the view that courts have the competence to create law, or should we give up the view that competence is a necessary condition for legal validity? I suggest that we refine the view that courts have the competence to create law. We might say, more specifically, that courts have a *limited* competence to create law when deciding cases, that such a limited competence to create law is very different from the competence of the legislature to create law by enacting statutes, and that therefore the view that courts have the competence to create law in this way does not contradict the view that the separation of powers doctrine concerns the competences of the government.

Of course, this leaves us with the problem of explaining why judicial law-making should be thought to be problematic from the point of view of the separation of powers doctrine in the first place. If judicial law-making does not amount to law-making in the sense contemplated by the separation of powers doctrine, why should judicial law-making be thought problematic at all? But perhaps we might say that the problem about judicial law-making, properly understood, is a democracy problem and not a separation of powers problem, in the sense that it is really about the fact that

---

[16] See, e.g., Trevor C. Hartley, 'The European Court, Judicial Objectivity and the Constitution of the European Union,' *Law Quarterly Review* 112 (1996), 95–109; Anthony Arnull, 'The European Court and Judicial Objectivity: A Reply to Professor Hartley,' *Law Quarterly Review* 112 (1996), 411–423; Takis Tridimas, 'The Court of Justice and Judicial Activism,' *European Law Review* 21 (1996) 199–210. See also United Steelworkers v. Weber, 443 US 193, 216–219 (1979) (Burger, J., dissenting).

[17] Trevor Hartley's critique of the European Court of Justice's willingness to decide cases outside or contrary to the natural meaning of the relevant provisions illustrates my understanding of judicial activism rather well. Hartley does not speak of 'judicial activism,' however. See Hartley, *The European Court.*

[18] For more on this topic, see Torben Spaak, *Guidance and Constraint: The Action-Guiding Capacity of Theories of Legal Reasoning* (Uppsala 2007) 271–274.

unlike legislators, judges are not responsible to the electorate.[19] Luckily, a closer investigation of this problem falls outside the scope of this article.

6 To Have Competence

To have competence, then, is to have the possibility, by performing a special kind of act, to change legal positions. To gain a better understanding of the nature of this possibility, we may distinguish between (i) competence as permission, (ii) competence as a practical possibility, and (iii) competence as (what we might call) a hypothetical possibility.[20] Let us treat these alternatives in this order.

To conceive of competence as a special case of *permission* is simply a mistake. Writers who maintain that competence should be analysed in terms of permission seem to be saying either (a) that competence *is* a permission, or (b) that competence *presupposes* permission.[21] The first alternative is difficult even to understand, and the second alternative does not comport with the facts. For we all know that a thief can sell stolen goods to a bona fide purchaser without being permitted to do so, and a person who is authorised to act on behalf of another can – but may not – act contrary to his instructions.[22] One might perhaps argue that in such a case the legal system somehow permits the agent to bring about a change of legal positions while also prohibiting him from exercising his competence. On this analysis, the agent would be prohibited from exercising his competence, while also being permitted to bring about the change of legal positions involved. But in my view, this way of putting it would create nothing but confusion. Note also that on this analysis, this norm-conflict would be a necessary – not only a contingent – feature of any legal system that in some situations prohibits the agent from exercising his competence.

To conceive of the competent person's possibility to change legal positions as a special case of practical possibility does not comport with the facts either. On this analysis, a person would not have the competence to draw up a will, say, if he were locked up in a room without writing equipment. But this is simply not how we conceive of the concept of legal competence: no one would say that a person in these circumstances lacks the competence to draw up a will. Interestingly, Lars Lindahl suggests that Hohfeld thought of the competent person's possibility to change legal positions along the lines of a practical possibility.[23] I believe, however, that

[19] See, e.g., Ronald Dworkin, *Taking Rights Seriously*. 2nd edition (London 1978) 84. I would like to thank Anders Fogelklou for discussing this question with me.
[20] I follow Lars Lindahl here. See Lindahl, *Position and Change*, 194. Lindahl does not, however, use the term 'hypothetical possibility'.
[21] See, e.g., Carlos E. Alchourrón and Eugenio Bulygin, *Normative Systems* (Wien and New York 1971) 151–152.
[22] For a fuller analysis of the relation between competence and permission, see Spaak, *The Concept of Legal Competence*, 80–87.
[23] Lindahl, *Position and Change*, 206–210.

Hohfeld – like most legal scholars – thought of this ability or possibility along the lines of (what I call) a hypothetical possibility.[24]

I believe instead that the correct understanding of the concept of possibility used in the definition of the competence concept above is alternative (iii): to have competence is to have a *hypothetical possibility* in the following sense: *if* the agent (in an adequate situation) performs a C-act (and thus goes about it in the right way), he brings about the intended change of position. And this is fully consistent with his not having the practical possibility to perform the C-act, perhaps because of physical impediment.[25]

We should note that there is a significant structural similarity between the concepts '(legal) competence' thus understood and '(physical) power,' and that therefore we may, and perhaps should, put the concept of (legal) competence on an equal footing with *dispositional* concepts such as abilities, character traits and the like.[26] The idea, then, is that a statement that the agent has legal competence in a certain respect should be understood, in principle, in the same way as a statement that he is irascible, intelligent or that he otherwise has some common (physical or mental) ability. Scholars have usually tried to explicate statements that ascribe dispositional characteristic to someone or something by saying that the agent or object, *if* certain special conditions exist, *will* behave in a certain way, that is, with the help of non truth-functional conditionals. If someone asks, for instance, what it means that a sugar cube is soluble in water, he will get the answer that *if* a sugar cube is submerged in water it does (as a matter of fact) dissolve (given certain additional conditions which we will disregard here). If, instead, someone asks what it means that a person has the competence to make a will, he will get the answer that *if* the person in question in an adequate situation performs a C-act, and thus goes about it in the right way, he will bring about a (valid) will.

I therefore suggest the following, improved definition of the concept of legal competence:

> (D.2) A person, p, has the competence in regard to a legal position, *LP*, if, and only if, there is a C-act, a, and a situation, S, such that if p in S performs a, and thus goes about it in the right way, p will, through a, change *LP*.

7 To Exercise Competence

To have competence is one thing, to *exercise* it is another. There are, however, a number of different ways in which a person can change legal positions, and the trick is to distinguish between those changes that result from the agent's exercise of his

---

[24] For more on this topic, see Spaak, *The Concept of Legal Competence*, 87–92.

[25] Ibid. 80–87. My analysis is inspired by Carl Wellman's analysis in Carl Wellman, *A Theory of Rights* (Totowa 1985) 47–48.

[26] This has been pointed out by Nils Kristian Sundby. See Nils Kristian Sundby, *Om normer* (Oslo-Bergen-Tromsø 1974) 335–337.

competence and those changes that result from his exercise of his general ability or power of changing legal positions.

First, we need to distinguish between competence and *Deliktsfähigkeit*, that is, the possibility of changing one's legal position by committing a crime or a tort. As I see it, the relevant difference is that whereas competence has been conferred on a person in order to give him the possibility, and in some circumstances also the duty, to change legal positions, the possibility of committing a delict is secondary to the aim of preventing certain types of act from ever being performed, in the sense that it is a *means* to that *end*. On this analysis, what is important are the *reasons* for conferring competence on a person compared with the reasons for giving him the possibility of changing legal positions by committing a crime or a tort. These reasons, it seems to me, must be the reasons (in the sense of the purpose) behind the statute in question that we can *rationally attribute to the legislature*. In my view, a rational legislature would enact a statute conferring competence on a class of persons in a certain respect, either because it believes that there is a moral value, such as individual liberty or autonomy, in letting those persons themselves determine their legal positions in the relevant respect, or because it believes that giving them this possibility helps making the law more flexible, or both. And, as I intimated above, I believe that a rational legislature would enact a criminal code, because it wants to prevent certain types of acts from ever being performed, or at least to minimise their occurrence. Since these are very different types of reason, it makes good sense to distinguish between competence and *Deliktsfähigkeit*.

True, not all legal norms are the result of legislation. We also have to take into account case law and customary law. But pure case law, which does not concern the interpretation of a statute, plays a negligible role in most contemporary legal systems,[27] and the same can be said about customary law. And mixed case law, which does concern the interpretation of a statute, does not, in this respect, add anything of interest to the statute, since it interprets precisely it. Moreover, if and insofar as the norms in question do *not* stem from legislation, we may think of the reasons behind them as the reasons that we could rationally attribute to the legislature, on the assumption that it had enacted them.

Second, we need to distinguish between competence and the possibility of changing one's legal position in regard to taxes and social benefits, among other things, by moving from one city to another. For the reason the law makes people's legal position to a certain extent dependent on their place of domicile is not that one wants to give them the possibility of bringing about the intended change of position by moving, but that it is generally reasonable that a person pays his taxes etc. where he lives. Thus, the same reasons that speak for *Deliktsfähigkeit* being kept out of the concept of competence also speak for certain other ways changing legal positions being kept outside of this concept.

---

[27] See Neil MacCormick, 'Why Cases Have *Rationes* and What These Are,' in: Laurence Goldstein (ed.), *Precedent in Law* (Oxford 1987) 155–182.

We have seen *why* we should delimit the concept of competence. There remains the question *how* we should go about doing that. I suggest that what is important is the agent's *mode of action* when bringing about the change of legal position. We can express this by saying that the agent exercises his competence by performing a *competence-exercising act*, or, for short, a C-act. If a person has the necessary competence, his performance (in the right manner and in the right situation) of a C-act constitutes a sufficient as well as a necessary condition for the intended legal effect. Hence if, and only if, we know when a person has performed a C-act, we know when he exercises (or tries to exercise) competence. That is to say, C-acts are our only clues in the search for legal effect and this means that it is important that we be clear about their characteristics.

What, then, are these characteristics? I suggest that a C-act is an action that depends for its legal effect on having been performed with the (actual or imputed) intent to bring about the said effect. As Neil MacCormick puts it, '[p]ower is conferred by a rule when the rule contains a condition which is satisfied only by an act performed with the (actual or imputed) intention of invoking the rule.'[28] As should be clear, the (actual or imputed) intent is a *necessary*, but not a sufficient, condition for the said effect – if the person performing a C-act is not legally qualified to do that (perhaps because he is a minor), then the legal effect will not ensue. So on a broad understanding of the concept of a declaration of intention (or *Willenserklärung*), we might say that the agent exercises his competence by performing a declaration of intention.[29]

If we conceive of the C-act in this way, we can easily distinguish between a case when a competent person exercises his competence and a case when he changes legal positions by committing a crime or a tort. In the former, but not the latter, case the change of legal positions presupposes an (actual or imputed) intent on the part of the agent to change the legal positions in question. In the latter, but not the former, case the agent does not have to intend to change the legal positions in question, although he must intend to bring about a factual state of affairs, say, to inflict pain on another person, or to cause damage to an object – if there is no such intent, there is no crime. The difference between the two cases, then, is that in the competence case the required intent concerns a question of *law*, whereas in the crime case it concerns a question of *fact*.

We see, then, that the analysis of the concept of a C-act in terms of the agent's (actual or imputed) intent to bring about the change of legal positions is very much in keeping with the reason given for distinguishing between a person's competence and his general ability or power of changing legal positions: If, as I have suggested,

---

[28] Neil MacCormick, *H. L. A. Hart* (Stanford 1981) 74. We see that this analysis is reminiscent of Paul Grice's well-known analysis of the concept of linguistic (or non-natural) *meaning*. On Grice's analysis, a person, *A*, *means* something by *x* if, and only if, *A* intends his utterance of *x* to mean something and intends the audience to recognise that he means something by uttering *x*. See Paul Grice, 'Meaning', *Philosophical Review* 66 (1957) 377–388.

[29] For a thorough analysis of the concept of a declaration of intention, Swedish speaking readers may wish to consult Ola Svensson, *Viljeförklaringen och dess innehåll* (Stockholm 1996).

a rational legislature would enact a statute conferring competence on a class of persons in a certain respect, either because it believes that there is a moral value, such as individual liberty or autonomy, in letting those persons themselves determine their legal positions in the relevant respect, or because it believes that giving them this possibility helps making the law more flexible, or both, then it is quite reasonable to make *p*'s exercise of his competence dependent on his (actual or imputed) intent to bring about the relevant legal effect.

On the basis of the above analysis, I therefore suggest the following, final definition of the concept of legal competence:

> (D.3) A person, *p*, has the competence in regard to a legal position, *LP*, if, and only if, there is a C-act, *a*, such that it depends for its legal effect on having been performed with an (actual or imputed) intent to bring about the relevant legal effect, and a situation, *S*, such that if *p* in *S* performs *a*, and thus goes about it in the right way, *p* will, through *a*, change *LP*.

8 Types of Competence

There are different types of legal competence. The most common and also the most conspicuous distinction is doubtless that between *autonomous* competence, which is competence to change legal positions in a way that binds the competent person himself, and *heteronomous* competence, which is competence to change legal positions in a way that that binds others.[30] This distinction exists in two different versions, and it is also somewhat unclear in other respects. Kelsen, for example, makes a distinction between autonomous and heteronomous competence, which he conceives of as a distinction between two ways of creating norms.[31] Ross, on the other hand, makes a distinction between private autonomy and public authority, which rests, or seems to rest, on four distinct criteria.[32] I believe, however, that we are justified in treating Kelsen's and Ross' distinctions as two versions of the same distinction, and that the important issue is whether or not the agent can obligate other persons without their consent.

The distinction between autonomous and heteronomous competence thus conceived is clearly morally relevant. Whereas a person's competence to obligate himself rarely gives rise to moral difficulties, a person's competence to obligate others typically does.[33] In the final analysis, the existence of heteronomous competence concerns the question of the moral legitimacy of the legal system.

---

[30] For more on this distinction, see Spaak, *The Concept of Legal Competence*, 128–134.

[31] Hans Kelsen, *General Theory of Law and State*. Trans. Anders Wedberg (Union, New Jersey 1999 [1945]) 203–205.

[32] Ross, *Directives*, 132–133.

[33] This assumes, of course, that one holds the view that human beings are born free and equal. However, I make precisely that assumption.

Other writers make a distinction between norm-creating and regulative competence.[34] Like the distinction between autonomous and heteronomous competence, this distinction exists in two different versions and is also somewhat unclear in other respects. Crudely put, *norm-creating* competence is a competence to create norms, whereas *regulative* competence is competence to change legal positions without creating norms. Examples of norm-creating competence include legislative power; as examples of regulative competence one might mention the government's competence to declare a state of emergency or to appoint judges, or a clergyman's competence to marry a couple.

While the distinction between norm-creating and regulative competence is less interesting from a moral point of view than the distinction between autonomous and heteronomous competence, it is more interesting from a norm-theoretical point of view. What is really interesting about this distinction is the precise nature of regulative competence. Joseph Raz, for example, maintains that regulative competence governs the application of pre-existing norms.[35] But, one might ask, can one really change a legal position without creating, modifying, or repealing a legal norm? Unfortunately, Raz does not explain just how the agent exercises this type of competence.

But perhaps we gain little by delving deeper into this problem. For we accept, of course, that legal norms attach legal effects to greatly different acts and events, such as different types of physical violence and the birth and death of human beings, and why, one might ask, should precisely those acts where the agent exercises regulative competence be seen as especially problematic? I am therefore inclined to believe that it suffices to note that to exercise regulative competence is to change legal positions, not by creating norms, but by regulating the application of already existing norms.

Finally, it is worth noting that having competence does not entail having a right, at least on the choice-theory of rights. A judge may have the competence to try certain types of case while being under an obligation to exercise this competence when a case of the relevant type is brought before him, and we have seen that a thief has the competence to sell stolen goods to a bona fide purchaser even though he is not permitted to do so. In neither case does the competent person have a right, according to the choice-theory. This is enough to show that having competence does not entail having a right, on this theory.[36]

---

[34] See, e.g. Joseph Raz, *The Concept of a Legal System*. 2nd edition (Oxford 1980); Sundby, *Om normer*, 361. For more on this topic, see Spaak, *The Concept of Legal Competence*, 134–143.

[35] Joseph Raz, 'Voluntary Obligations and Normative Powers,' *The Aristotelian Society. Supplementary Volume XLVI* (1972), 79–102, at 82.

[36] For more on this topic, see Spaak, *The Concept of Legal Competence*, 143–151.

9 The Adequacy of the Proposed Explication

I said above (in Section 3) that an explication of a concept, that is, the *explicatum*, is adequate if, and only if, it is (i) similar to the *explicandum* as well as (ii) exact, (iii) fruitful, and (iv) simple, and that I think of my analysis of the concept of legal competence as an explication of the concept of legal competence described by Hohfeld, Kelsen, Ross, and Hart.

I believe my explication satisfies these four conditions. As I see it, the *explicatum*, as I have defined it (D.3 in Section 7), is (i) similar to the *explicandum*, that is, the concept of legal competence described by the above-mentioned authors. It is (ii) if not exact, then at least more exact than the *explicandum*, in that it incorporates the idea of hypothetical possibility, the idea of a C-act, and the idea of a situation in which the agent performs the C-act, as well as a more refined understanding of the concept 'change of legal positions'. It is (iii) fruitful, though not necessarily more fruitful than the *explicandum,* in that it can be used not only to analyse and discuss questions of legal validity and invalidity both in the particular case and in general, but also to detect similarities and differences between such questions in different legal fields. And it is (iv) simple, almost as simple as the *explicandum.*

As should be clear (see Section 3), the satisfaction by the proposed explication of these four conditions does not mean that the explication is in any sense true, but only that it is *useful* for a certain purpose, in this case (as we have seen) to analyse and discuss questions about legal validity and invalidity.

Acknowledgments I would like to thank Brian Bix, Åke Frändberg, Cyril Holm, Thomas Mautner, Dennis Patterson, and Lennart Åqvist for helpful comments on an earlier version of the article. I also would like to thank Sven Ove Hansson as well as the editors of this volume for helpful comments and suggestions in the final stages of preparation. In addition, I would like to thank the participants in the special workshop 'General Concepts in the Law' at the IVR conference in Krakau, Poland 1–6 August 2007, for helpful comments on my presentation of some of the ideas put forward in the article. The usual caveat applies, however: The author alone is responsible for any remaining mistakes and imperfections. Note also that Sections 4, 6, 7, and 8 in this article draw heavily on the analysis in Torben Spaak, *The Concept of Legal Competence* (Dartmouth 1994) Chs. 1, 4, and 5.

The Influence of Normative Reasons on the Formation of Legal Concepts

Lorenz Kähler

1 Introduction

Legal concepts are an odd entity. While on the one side a key element of the law they are also embedded in ordinary language. So it is, at first glance, unclear whether they have a legal, a semantic or a dual nature. This background is particularly important for two questions which every legal system needs to answer. The first is which concepts to use. The second is how to define them. The answer to both questions is what I will call the formation of legal concepts. It is central for the understanding of how legal concepts emerge and develop. This paper will try to shed some light on it by asking whether it is influenced by normative reasons. From the outset it seems obvious that they play, at least, some role in the choice and definition of legal concepts. For what else could determine which concepts a legislator should choose and how he should define them? The definition of property, for instance, depends inter alia on considerations which kind of material and immaterial things he wants to protect. However, it is far from obvious that there are no other factors that play a role in it. Possibly, semantic laws are to be considered, too. Moreover, even if normative reasons are decisive for the formation of legal concepts it is still an open question whether any normative reason can play a role in it or whether some kinds of them are excluded.

To understand the role of normative reasons, I will first need to explore which influence they have on the formation of legal concepts. As it turns out, there are several independent aspects in which normative reasons play a role (Section 2). Once their effect becomes evident the question is how far it will go. I will argue that there are constraints against their effect and that these are essential for understanding the formation of legal concepts. The introduction of new concepts, for instance, is counter-balanced by the risk that these concepts cause misunderstanding. Although the legislator is free to introduce new concepts with regard to its political program,

L. Kähler (✉)
University of Göttingen, Göttingen, Germany
e-mail: lkaehler@web.de

J.C. Hage, D. von der Pfordten (eds.), *Concepts in Law*, Law and Philosophy Library 88,
DOI 10.1007/978-90-481-2982-9_6, © Springer Science+Business Media B.V. 2009

there are reasons against using such concepts. So, at least, not any normative reason can determine the choice and definition of legal concepts (Section 3).

Before I get into these questions, some remarks on terminology are necessary: I speak about 'concept formation' rather than 'concept construction'. 'Concept construction' suggests a conscious process, whereas the process in which legal concepts are established is not necessarily an intentional one. The legislator might use certain concepts without knowing why they are preferable to others. Like concepts used in everyday language,[1] legal concepts may evolve gradually in an unconscious manner. For this reason, the term 'concept formation' is to be used for both conscious and unconscious processes.

Secondly, I will use 'normative reason' in a broad sense as to include any reason capable of prescribing an action or evaluation.[2] For instance, if people constantly mix up one particular concept with another one then this could be used as a reason against its usage. Normative reasons are not confined to 'moral' or 'ethical' reasons. These are the most prominent, though not the only, kind of normative reasons and include considerations with respect to prevailing conventional morality as well as justifiable, critical morality.[3] In addition, there are other existing normative reasons. Among them are, for instance, aesthetical considerations regarding the symmetry of a conceptual scheme.

Not any reason for a certain choice or definition of a legal concept is a normative reason. For not all reasons are capable of prescribing an action or evaluation. There are, what Dancy calls, 'enticing reasons' about what is fun, amusing or enjoyable. They are reasons for an action but cannot generate an ought.[4] For the mere fact that somebody likes a concept is not sufficient to establish that people have to use it. This has an important implication. If the choice and definition of legal concepts depend, at least in part, on normative reasons, they are not just a matter of convenience, as it is sometimes suggested.[5] Moreover, reasonable disagreement about the choice and definition of concepts becomes possible too. For different people have different values and attitudes that influence which normative reasons they consider as valid. Contrary to that, natural kind concepts like 'water' or 'tiger' are determined by facts that are independent on the values and attitudes of the people referring to them. Reasonable disagreement hence could occur only in the way to discover these facts. But in the definition of these concepts no normative reason would play a role. In that

[1] See for the unconscious evolution of language H.J. Heringer, 'Sprache, Sprachkritik – und Ethik', in: J. Berendes (ed.), *Autonomie durch Verantwortung* (Paderborn 2007) 442; G. Orrigi and D. Sperber, 'Evolution, communication, and the proper function of language', in: P. Carruthers and A. Chamberlain (eds.), *Evolution and the Human Mind* (Cambridge 2000) 140.

[2] See for a broad understanding of normative reasons: C. Halbig, *Praktische Gründe und die Realität der Moral* (Frankfurt 2007) 6, 113; J. Raz, 'Explaining Normativity: On Rationality and the Justification of Reason', in: J. Dancy (ed.), *Normativity* (Oxford 2000) 34.

[3] For the distinction, see H.L.A. Hart, *Law, Liberty, and Morality* (Oxford 1968) 20.

[4] J. Dancy, 'Nonnaturalism', in: D. Copp (ed.), *Oxford Handbook of Ethical Theory* (Oxford 2005) 135.

[5] See e.g. K. Röhl, *Allgemeine Rechtslehre* (Köln 2001) 35; L. Lindahl, 'Deduction and Justification in the Law. The Role of Legal Terms and Concepts', *Ratio Juris* 2004, 186.

sense it would be neutral. If the definition of legal concepts, however, is influenced by normative reasons it cannot be such a descriptive enterprise. It would not be sufficient to refer to some natural fact and to maintain that it is the defining feature of the concept.

Finally, legal concepts are understood broadly to include all concepts used in legal rules, either as part of the rule conditions, or as part of the rule consequences, if their content is governed by legal rules.[6] Examples for such concepts are equality, freedom of speech, property, or possession. The question whether normative reasons might influence the way concepts are formed is related but not identical to the debate on the normativity of language. This debate concerns the question whether there is a correct usage of words and what this correctness may be.[7] However, the question I will deal with is which reasons govern the introduction and definition of concepts, and not the subsequent question of what it means to use the words with which they are expressed correctly.

2 How Normative Reasons Influence the Formation of Legal Concepts

In the selection of legal concepts the legislator has three options: He might deploy already established concepts, modify them, or use new ones. The choice of established concepts seems preferable if they have a clear-cut meaning and are used within a known setting. It makes little sense, for instance, to introduce a new concept for driving license unless the concept in current use is causing difficulties. Contrary to that, the modification of old concepts or the introduction of new concepts is a frequent phenomenon in developing fields like the internet. So the legislator might, for instance, use the established concept of property to describe the rights and duties of a domain-holder. But he might also introduce the new concept of 'domain holding' and distinguish it from property ownership. With the exception of constitutional provisions requiring the comprehensibility of legal rules,[8] neither ordinary language nor the existing law dictates his choice. The two do not exclude the introduction of new concepts or the modification of established ones.

Once a number of options for the selection of concepts exist the question arises whether their choice is to be determined by normative reasons. If such reasons do not exist the choice of legal concepts would be either arbitrary, if there are no reasons for that choice at all, or neutral, if these reasons are descriptive in kind. It would in any case not depend on moral or aesthetic considerations. There are several ways in

[6] A broader understanding is used by R. Dworkin, *Justice in Robes* (Cambridge, Mass. 2006) 223, who writes about 'concepts of law' as any 'concepts people use to talk about law'.

[7] See R. Brandom, *Making It Explicit* (Cambridge, Mass. 1994) 30; P. Horwich, *Meaning* (Oxford 2004) 184.

[8] That is one consequence the German constitutional court 'Bundesverfassungsgericht' draws from the rule of law, *Neue Juristische Wochenschrift* 1967, 619.

which one could claim that legal concepts are independent upon normative reasons and in this sense neutral. At least, four claims must be distinguished:

1) Normative reasons do not follow from legal concepts (*neutral consequences thesis*).
2) Normative reasons do not determine the choice of legal concepts (*neutral choice thesis*).
3) Normative reasons do not determine the content of legal concepts (*neutral content thesis*).
4) Normative reasons do not determine the process how legal concepts are defined (*neutral process thesis*).

According to thesis 1, concepts by their nature do not prescribe actions and can, therefore, not have normative implications. Legal consequences can follow only from a rule encapsulating such concepts. So the mere fact that a proposition uses a concept is insufficient to draw any normative conclusion. The concept of property, for instance, does not imply rights or duties of the owner. A legal system might grant the owner certain rights, as is the case in free market economies, or might in their absence form the basis of heavy taxation, as was the case in socialist countries. From the knowledge which legal concepts a legal system deploys does not follow which actions it ultimately prohibits or allows.[9] More generally, the normative nature of legal rules does not imply that their concepts are chosen and defined according to certain normative reasons. This is even true of deontic concepts like 'duty' or 'right'. Although their application in a particular instance has to be justified by normative reasons, no normative implication follows from the mere fact that the law uses them. It might, for instance, deploy them positively to state some duty or formulate negatively that no duty arises in a particular situation. This hence lends support to the first thesis.

This thesis is further supported by the fact that the law frequently uses evaluatively indeterminate concepts. These are concepts that can be used both to approve and repudiate a situation or an action. Without an evaluation a concept is incapable of prescribing an action or an evaluation. The concept of possession, for instance, does not include a judgment over whether the control over the possessed object is legal or illegal, moral or immoral. However that may be, the law refers to it as the possession of an object. Similarly, the fact that a certain organisation is a state says little about its character. It might be a democracy as well as a dictatorship, a member of the UN as well as a rogue state, one that respects human rights or one that disregards them. Although these properties influence the normative evaluation of the state they are not part of its concept. Such concepts are thus evaluatively

[9] Cf. B. Brouwer and J. Hage, 'Basic Concepts of European Private Law', *European Review of Private Law*, 15 (2007), 6: 'The adoption of a set of basic concepts has relatively little influence on the law'; K. Füßer, 'Farewell to "Legal Positivism": The Separation Thesis Unravelling', in: R. George (ed.), *The Autonomy of Law* (Oxford 1996) 142, discussing the 'Anti-Commitment Thesis' of legal concepts. On the independence of concepts and actions see S. Körner, 'On Some Moral and Other Concepts', *Philosophy and Phenomenological Research* 1950, 184.

indeterminate. Therefore, one cannot deduct from them a reason how to evaluate the entity to which they refer, let alone a reason how to act. For without a positive evaluation of an action the law cannot require it.[10] This demonstrates neither that concepts like state or property are morally neutral nor that they are beyond dispute. There is a difference between a concept being morally neutral and one that is evaluatively indeterminate. But it does show that legal consequences do not follow from concepts alone and that there is no necessary link between a legal concept and the legal or moral evaluation of the situation to which it applies. This might explain how it is possible that different legal systems use equivalent concepts[11] despite the tremendous political, economic and ideological differences between them.

The frequent use of evaluatively indeterminate legal concepts is far from self-evident. Theoretically, the law could use evaluatively determinate concepts, depending on how an action or situation is assessed. For legally acquired goods, it may use, for instance, the concept of property whereas illegally acquired items are attributed the concept of 'i-property'. Similarly, it might refute the usage of the concept of state and speak instead of either democracies or dictatorships. In this manner Aristotle distinguishes between monarchy and tyranny, aristocracy and oligarchy, democracy and timocracy.[12] Each pair represents a dichotomy, one being the ideal, the other the degenerated antipode. Similarly, political concepts frequently distinguish people or situations by their normative merits. So a 'terrorist' differs from a 'freedom fighter' insofar as the former's actions are condemned while the activities of the latter are praised, irrespective of the fact that both these individual's actions might be carried out in exactly the same way, e.g. setting off bombs. Unlike evaluatively indeterminate concepts, there is no opportunity to distinguish between good and bad terrorism. To speak of terrorists is to condemn them. Using evaluatively determinate concepts has the advantage that the overall-evaluation is clearly discernible. But it comes with the disadvantage that one has to use a different concept if one's evaluation changes.

Conversely, legal concepts like 'property' or 'possession' lack easy labelling, as being either evaluatively positive or negative. They seldom follow the Aristotelian model of concept definition. So to know whether a certain object is the property of someone does not determine whether he is allowed or entitled to use it. Though he might be the rightful owner, he might also have the obligation to confer it to someone else. Moreover, the knowledge that someone is in possession of property leaves the evaluation of this situation open. One could condemn or approve of it. Hence the application of these concepts is independent of the normative merits of the situation to which they apply. This does not preclude that theories shaping legal concepts may at the same time influence the rules in which they occur.[13] But then

---

[10] Otherwise a performative contradiction would arise; see R. Alexy, *Theorie der juristischen Argumentation* (Frankfurt am Main 1983) 428.

[11] For this equivalence see S. Šarčević, *New approach to legal translation* (The Hague 1997) 234.

[12] Aristotle, *Nicomachische Ethik* (G. Bien (ed.), Hamburg 1985), 1160a–1161a; Politik (G. Bien (ed.), Hamburg 1990), 1279a 17.

[13] Cf. G. Sartor, *Legal Reasoning* (Dordrecht 2005) 563.

it is the theories and not their concepts that have normative implications. Separately taken, legal concepts can generate neither a reason how to evaluate a situation nor a reason how to act. The neutral consequence thesis thus seems correct.

The veracity of thesis 1 does not automatically imply the veracity of thesis 2, according to which normative reasons do not determine the choice of legal concepts. Although normative reasons do not follow from legal concepts they may still influence what concepts should be chosen. For not all legal concepts may be equally suitable for prescribing behaviour via legal rules. If all concerned people understand concepts A, B and C in a specific way due to their foundation in ordinary language or common practice, it is preferable to use them rather than the more abstract concept of D that contains A, B and C.[14] Equally, if concept E is well established and has a clear meaning its usage might be preferable to the deployment of a new concept, F, which though more precise than E may cause misunderstanding and unwanted interpretations. Concepts can thus vary in their suitability for deployment within legal rules, whose aims are to bring about certain legal consequences. The reasons for these consequences might therefore indirectly influence the choice of a legal concept. For if these reasons require that under certain conditions certain legal consequences shall occur and if particular concepts are most suitable to formulate such a rule, then these reasons also support their use. They are then the best means to realise one's aims.

Moreover, normative reasons might exclude certain concepts because of their affiliation with a particular ideology or political program,[15] even if they fit well into the legal rules and the consequences these rules are expected to bring about. The concept of 'European citizenship', for instance, is clearly preferable to the concept of 'European race' because the former is free of the impression that there is something like a biologically distinguishable 'European race' on which the European Union is founded. Nevertheless, such a concept might be adopted in place of 'European citizenship' without inducing any change in the conditions under which the legal consequences occur. Normative reasons can hence determine the choice of concepts equally suitable to be employed in a certain legal rule. Their choice is, therefore, governed by more than considerations with respect to the consequences legal rules shall have. These consequences are central for the law, but not the only aspect that counts.

A similar picture emerges in the decision of how legal concepts are defined. If this decision were free from normative reasons the neutral content thesis 3 would then be correct. It is neither implied by the neutral choice thesis 2 nor can it be refuted by showing thesis 2 to be incorrect. For one could argue that legal concepts, once chosen in accordance to normative principles, should be defined without reference to

---

[14] Besides that, the general concept would be less precise; for the conflict between precision and abstraction of concepts, see G. Sartori, 'Concept Misformation in Comparative Politics', *American Political Science Review*, 64 (1970) 1033.

[15] For examples how the change of concepts indicates historical changes see M. Richter, 'Conceptualizing the Contestable: "Begriffsgeschichte" and Political Concepts', in: G. Scholz (ed.), *Die Interdisziplinarität der Begriffsgeschichte* (Hamburg 2000) 141.

any normative reason. Their definition would in this case depend only on descriptive propositions. Thesis 2 would thus be incorrect while thesis 3 correct. But this state of affair, although logically possible, is implausible. Both questions are related. Rather than using a new concept, the law could instead redefine an existing one. In both cases it is decisive whether the concepts are capable to state the conditions under which the required legal consequences shall occur. The decision how to define concepts resembles thus the choice how to define them. If thesis 2 is incorrect, then thesis 3 could hardly be correct. So if, for instance, normative reasons require to use the concept 'real property' instead of the concept 'property' because of its limited scope, then they also exclude that 'real property' is defined in such a broad way as to include any movable and immovable right.

If the opposite holds and normative reasons could not influence the definition of legal concepts, it would not play a role whether a definition was brief and concise, or long and verbose. For the preference for brief and concise definitions is normative in kind. If such considerations were excluded, any definition could be used. But this contradicts with the fact that such definitions are more suitable to further the aims of the law. Equally, concepts that are part of a consistent and coherent conceptual scheme are easier to handle than overlapping ad-hoc classifications.[16] There are hence normative reasons that influence how legal concepts shall be defined. Because of that a good deal of scholarly work has been invested in the defining of legal concepts.

Finally, as with the choice of legal concepts, there might be normative reasons against certain definitions because of their implicit values or ideological connotations.[17] Most of the time such definitions are unsuitable as the rules using them would not have the required conditions of application and hence not the required consequences. The implementation of a discriminatory concept, for instance, would lead to excessively narrow results, since it would lack the breadth to encompass all states of affairs in which these consequences shall occur. So the definition of citizens as human beings over 40 years of age would undermine a regulation of democratic elections which shall be free of ageism. But even if the definition of a legal concept fits well to the required consequences, normative reasons against its deployment are imaginable. They might oppose the implied values and ideological connotations of these concepts. Concept could suggest a classification contrary to common perception or morality.

An example of such a concept can be found in the definition of 'things' (corporal objects) in German private law ('Sachen'). For over 90 years, the German civil code, the BGB, regarded animals as things. Animals were included in their implicit definition and the rules for things applied directly to them. In 1990 legislators changed this definition and stated: 'Animals are not things.'[18] However, his modification to the

[16] Cf. N. Stavropoulos, *Objectivity in Law* (Oxford 1996) 197.

[17] For connotations of words in general see S. Löbner, *Semantik* (Berlin 2003) 48.

[18] §90a BGB introduced by Art. 1 No 2, 'Gesetz zur Verbesserung der Rechtsstellung des Tieres im Bürgerlichen Recht' from 20th August 1990, *Bundesgesetzblatt I*, 1762. For § 90a BGB § 285a of the Austrian AGBG played the role model, see G. Mühe, 'Das Gesetz zur Verbesserung der

definition was not supposed to alter the conditions under which legal consequences occur and, as before, the same rules apply to animals and to things. The ownership of an animal is transferred in the same way as the ownership of tables, stones and cars. The legislators merely wished to avoid the impression that animals are nothing but corporal objects. For the present context it is not important whether this act of symbolic legislation is right. What is important is that there is a normative reason against a particular definition, namely the perception of animals as things, and that this reason is not based on the legal consequences of the rules using the concept. This example is another sign that thesis 3 is incorrect.

The question whether the neutral definition thesis 3 is correct ultimately rests on the question of what determines the content of legal concepts, i.e. how they are defined. In general the legislator can use a lexical, a stipulative or a real definition.[19] With a lexical definition he refers to the previous usage of the speech community or a certain practice within it.[20] Alternatively he might determine a concept solely by his own stipulative definition.[21] No further reference to convention or natural and social facts[22] would be needed. The definition could not be wrong. Lastly, with a real definition a natural property becomes decisive that exists independent of one's own view as well as the previously held conventions.[23] This property delimitates the extension as well as the intension of the concept. For instance, if the concept of a tiger is determined by a certain set of DNA, every animal that has such a DNA would be a tiger. Even an animal previously thought to be a cat could turn out to be one.[24] It would not matter that people used to classify it differently. All that counts are the real properties.

Can legal concepts be defined in the same way? Are there real definitions of legal and political concepts? According to Dworkin, there are, at least, 'instructive similarities' between such concepts and natural kinds.[25] Central political and legal

---

Rechtsstellung des Tieres im bürgerlichen Recht', *Neue Juristische Wochenschrift* 1990, 2238, 2239.

[19] Others distinguish between real and nominal definitions, see C.G. Hempel, *Fundamentals of Concept Formation in Empirical Science* (Chicago 1952) 2. In this account nominal definitions include stipulative as well as lexical definitions. Fur further classifications of definitions see J. Sager, *A Practical Course in Terminology Processing* (Amsterdam, Philadelphia 1990) 42.

[20] See P. Hanna and B. Harrison, *Word World* (Cambridge 2004) 58, 213; R. Robinson, *Definition* (Oxford 1950) 35.

[21] Robinson, *Definition*, 59.

[22] J. Searle, *The Construction of Social Reality* (New York 1995) 31, 59.

[23] See Robinson, *Definition*, 149; Hempel, *Fundamentals of Concept Formation*, 6; T. Pawlowski, *Concept Formation in the Humanities and Social Sciences* (Dordrecht 1980) 48.

[24] For a critique see D. Patterson, 'Dworkin on the Semantics of Legal and Political Concepts', *Oxford Journal of Legal Studies*, 26 (2006) 552, arguing that the meaning of a concept cannot be a function of hidden essences.

[25] R. Dworkin, 'Hart's Postscript and the Character of Political Philosophy', *Oxford Journal of Legal Studies*, 24 (2004) 12. For a critique, see Patterson, *Dworkin on the Semantics of Legal and Political Concepts*, 546.

concepts, like equality, are determined by political philosophy.[26] They are similar to the natural kinds insofar that neither their existence nor their character depends on anyone's belief or decision. Both have of a deep structure that explains their 'concrete manifestations'.[27] If this were true of legal concepts, an objective property would determine their content. Their definition would be a descriptive enterprise. For the content of the concept would already be fixed by what Dworkin calls their 'deep structure', as the concept of tigers is fixed by their DNA. In keeping with this notion, Dworkin maintains that a scientist pursuing research to reveal the nature of a tiger differs only in degree from a political philosopher who strives to reveal the nature of liberty.[28]

However, Dworkin's account does not exclude that normative reasons are decisive for the definition of legal concepts. According to him, political concepts 'cannot be shown to be descriptive on the model of scientific investigation into natural kinds.'[29] They are interpretive and depend thus, at least partially, upon the interpreter or interpretive community.[30] Therefore, his theory can hardly exclude that normative reasons determine the content of legal concepts. For a decision between competing claims about the right interpretation of central legal and political concepts can only be solved by normative reasons. They show what a community shall regard as best for its own practices.

Moreover, even if legal concepts have an 'objective structure', as Dworkin maintains, normative reasons might still shape their content. For this structure might itself consist of normative reasons or, as Dworkin suggests,[31] of values that give rise to such reasons. In being described, neither the reasons nor their underlying values experience change to their normative status. If, for instance, equality demands that everyone be treated with equal respect, as Dworkin maintains,[32] the 'deep structure' of equality must therefore support reasons upholding this demand. Otherwise the demand of equal respect could not be justified. Hence, even if Dworkin's claim regarding the objective deep structure of central legal and political concepts is correct, normative reasons might still determine their content. Thus Dworkin's claim

---

[26] For Dworkin there is hardly a difference between central legal concepts and political concepts. For jurisprudence is for him 'an exercise in substantive political morality', *Hart's Postscript*, 31.

[27] Dworkin, *Hart's Postscript*, 12. For another account of legal concepts as real kinds see Brink, 'Legal Theory, Legal Interpretation, and Judicial Review', *Philosophy and Public Affairs*, 17(1988) 105; Stavropoulos, *Objectivity in Law*, 46, 89 who instead of 'deep structure' refers to their 'semantic depth'. For a critique see B. Bix, 'Can Theories of Meaning and Reference Solve the Problem of Legal Determinacy', *Ratio Juris*, 16 (2003) 281, arguing that such theories neglect authority of the law; Patterson, *Dworkin on Semantics*, 545.

[28] Dworkin, *Hart's Postscript*, 13.

[29] Dworkin, *Hart's Postscript*, 11. He even criticises positivist claims that law has an essential structure, *Justice in Robes*, 215. In 'Hart and the Concept of Law', *Harvard Law Review Forum*, 119 (2006) 98, Dworkin stresses that legal systems entail 'social kinds'.

[30] Dworkin, *Justice in Robes*, 225–227; see also Dworkin, *Hart's Postscript*, 25; *Law's Empire* (Cambridge 1986) 45.

[31] Dworkin, *Hart's Postscript*, 13.

[32] R. Dworkin, *Taking Rights Seriously* (London 1977) 272.

regarding the objective deep structure of legal concepts does not contradict the claim that normative reasons determine the content of legal concepts, although it does contradict the additional claim that these reasons depend solely on interpretation.[33]

Apart from this, normative reasons might influence the way legal concepts are defined. Procedural reasons can require the definition to be kept open to discussion and revision. They are normative in kind, because they require the participants of the legal discourse to behave in a certain way. So thesis 4 seems incorrect independently on whether thesis 3 is correct. The latter is an ontological thesis and concerned with the nature of legal concepts, while thesis 4 touches on the methodology of their definition. The distinction between them can be easily overlooked since the word 'definition' can mean both the content and the process of definition.[34] So even if the content of legal concepts is objectively determined, normative reasons can still influence the procedure of their definition. This is especially important due to the lack of an agreed upon methodology[35] on how to investigate and define legal concepts. For especially then normative principles have to guide this process.[36] They might, for instance, demand that no definition of a legal concept can be formulated without regard to tradition, investigation of the underlying principles and their likely empirical consequences, or that the definitions, once formulated, shall be updated[37] on a regular basis. These requirements neither prescribe nor exclude content of any sort, instead they determine the process. Nevertheless, they are normative in kind. So thesis 4 is as theses 2 and 3 incorrect.

3 Constraints on the Influence of Normative Reasons

The result that normative reasons influence the formation of legal concepts suggests that moral and political considerations could play a role in it. For once this process is normative in kind it becomes, at first glance, difficult to see why such considerations could be excluded a priori. They are, after all, normative in kind. But is there nothing behind the claim that legal concepts shall be impartially or neutrally defined?

To answer this question it is important to see that the refutations of theses 2, 3 and 4 neither show that the formation of concepts is always governed by normative

---

[33] Patterson, *Dworkin on Semantics,* 556, argues in general that in Dworkin's theory the interpretive aspect of 'fit' (accordance with previous usage) withers.

[34] R. Alexy, *Begriff und Geltung des Rechts* (Freiburg 1994) 40; Füßer, *Farewell to 'Legal Positivism'*, 133.

[35] Patterson, *Dworkin on Semantics*, 553.

[36] These principles may, but need not accord to an inferentialist account of concept's, see D. Canala and G. Tuzet, 'On Legal Inferentialism. Toward a Pragmatics of Semantic Content in Legal Interpretation', *Ratio Juris* 2007, 32, 40; Lindahl, *Deduction and Justification in the Law*, 193. For a general critique see: J. Fodor, 'Concepts; A Potboiler', *Philosophical Issues*, (1995) 10, 22.

[37] See R. Arntz, H. Picht, and F. Mayer, *Einführung in die Terminologiearbeit*, 4th edition (Hildesheim 2002) 69.

reasons,[38] nor prove that all normative reasons can influence it. The formation of legal concepts might, conversely, be hampered by constraints. By this I mean in a broad sense all factors, due to which normative reasons are either not decisive, or play a minor role in the formation of legal concepts. These constraints need not restrict their influence altogether. It is sufficient that they impede these normative reasons. In order to understand the variety of these constraints, it is useful to distinguish four kinds: linguistic, operational, functional, and benefit constraints.

3.1 Linguistic Constraints

Legal concepts must be expressed in words because they could otherwise not play a role in law or, arguably,[39] even exist. Although this is obvious, it has important repercussions for legal concepts. Due to the necessary formulation of concepts into words, constraints to their formation might in turn impact on the formation of concepts. Therefore it is worthwhile to take a brief look at the constraints of word formation.

In order to be understandable words must observe the phonological, semantic and syntactic rules of the ordinary language in which they are formulated. For instance, they cannot consist of new morphemes without threatening confusion.[40] The majority of the people would otherwise not be able to read or understand them. Similarly, words should not infringe the established syntactic, semantic and pragmatic rules of the ordinary language. Consequently, the number of communicable words in which legal concepts can be expressed is limited.[41] Therefore, one has either to express different concepts with the same words in which case these words acquire a multitude of meanings (polysemy[42]) or one has to limit the number of used concepts.

Even if it is possible to introduce a new word for a new concept, its application might become burdensome. New words tend to be longer than already existing ones. They must rely on complex combinations of existing morphemes so that it is more difficult to understand them and to commit them to memory.[43] Judges and other lawyers need more time and effort to use them. They cannot fall back on past

---

[38] Cf. Brouwer and Hage, *Basic Concepts*, 3.

[39] At least, Davidson argues that 'only a creature that can interpret speech can have the concept of a thought', *Inquiries into Truth and Interpretation* (Oxford 2001) 170. For M. Dummett, *The Seas of Language* (Oxford 1993) 97, the understanding of a word is the prototypical or even required case of the grasping of a concept.

[40] Cf. the requirements of terminology creation, A. Štambuk, 'The Norm and the Language of Science' in: P. Sandrini (ed.), *TKE '99 Terminology and Knowledge Engineering* (Vienna 1999) 105.

[41] This, of course, is true of word formation in general, see P. Ackema and A. Neeleman, *Beyond Morphology* (Oxford 2004) 2, 48, arguing that beyond morphological constraints there are syntactical and phonological constraints.

[42] Löbner, *Semantik*, 60.

[43] J. Gerring, '*What Makes a Concept Good? A Criterial Framework for Understanding Concept Formation in the Social Sciences*', published under www.highbeam.com (25-07-2007).

experience and an established, common understanding. Instead they need to figure out what the new terminology means. Misunderstanding is a possible result.

Similar difficulties occur with new combinations of already existing words. Because of semantic and syntactic rules, the possibilities are limited. If, for instance, two existing words are combined to form a new word, the one usually ends up specifying the other. A 'tort claim' would mean a claim that arises as a result of a tort. Theoretically, the law could define it differently, such as a claim arising without a tort. But such deviant usage would lead to confusion for all those concerned and would thus fail to advance the aims of the law.[44] Consequently, terminology constraints also limit the choice of legal concepts. For if no suitable word can be found to express a particular concept, then the concept cannot find common understanding and ultimately will not be used.

This limitation might be one reason why completely new concepts seldom emerge in law. The number of existing words is limited and the creation of new ones difficult. Even if new words are used, it is difficult to predict how they will be understood and interpreted across the legal community. For this reason, it is more usual to modify existing words in order to have their meanings extended than to invent new words.[45] Not surprisingly, among the vast quantity of legal concepts there are relatively few that do not have an equivalent in ordinary language.[46] This is a sign that linguistic constraints might influence the choice of concepts[47] and at the same time hamper the influence of normative reasons. For if ordinary language were richer and contained more possibilities to express and communicate ideas in word form, the variety of legal concepts would increase accordingly.

3.2 Operational Constraints

The influence of normative reasons might further be constrained by the difficulties they cause in the application of legal concepts. As we saw,[48] there is no reason why concepts should not have a clear evaluation of the facts to which they refer. However the application of such concepts is burdensome. The normative evaluation of objects, acts, and situations usually depends on a variety of factors like the actor's intent, her previous commitments, the consequences of the action, etc., so that the deployment of a concept based on a normative evaluation is cumbersome. If, for

---

[44] For the combination of concepts see G. Murphy, *The Big Book of Concepts* (Cambridge 2004) 465.

[45] Murphy, *The Big Book of Concepts*, 406; similarly, in the social sciences the stretching of concepts takes place, Gerring, *What Makes a Concept Good?*; Sartori, *Concept Misformation*, 1033.

[46] Lindahl, *Deduction and Justification*, 195. See also J. Gerring and P. Barresi, 'Putting Ordinary Language to Work', *Journal of Theoretical Politics*, 15 (2003) 222: 'Virtually all of the key terms of the social sciences are adapted from natural language.'; Löbner, *Semantik*, 60.

[47] Vice versa, the formation of words and terms might be limited by a systematisation of concepts, Sager, *A Practical Course in Terminology Processing*, 14.

[48] Section 2.

instance, the concept of property depends on the person who most deserves a certain object, it would be enormously difficult and controversial to declare who the rightful owner is. One would need to examine the various interests of all the parties affected before a decision, to whom it belongs, could be arrived at.

Moreover, when one uses evaluatively determinate concepts, one would frequently need to use one concept for the statement of facts and another concept for the statement of law, since the application of such concepts depends on the situation that is to prevail rather than on the actual prevailing situation. Thus the concepts would lose their suitability to describe the facts to which the law is to be applied. If legislators, for instance, were to define a state as a sovereign organisation which completely abided by human rights, they would have to use a different concept for the existing states. For all states at one time or another, and to certain degrees, infringe on human rights. Hence the application of concepts based on normative evaluations is more complex and troublesome. Concepts not based on them, though logically not required, are easier to deal with.

Similar reasons support the usage of already existing concepts despite possible normative reasons for the introduction of new ones. People accustomed to the old concepts have greater difficulties using new or modified ones and the chance of mistakes occurring in their application is more frequent. If a statute defined, for instance, a car as a vehicle travelling on two or more wheels, the probability that judges would not apply it to bicycles would be rather high. For though bicycles came under the new definition, the common perception would still be that they are not cars. At the very least, the interpretation of the concept becomes more burdensome, for one must either get used to the new concept or recheck its definition in the process of application.

Conversely, existing concepts are understood more easily than a newly introduced one. Due to an established practice, they do not require explicit definitions. For this reason, they are easier to adapt with respect to unforeseen circumstances. When they do occur, judges can maintain that the concepts are narrower or broader than they first appeared and might find analogies from earlier applications. However were they to have to apply newly defined concepts, the judges would be obliged to go by the new definition. If it fails to provide for exceptions, it could hardly be adapted to unanticipated situations. Therefore, legislators frequently abstain from defining concepts, preferring to rely instead on established concepts that can be modified in the legal process. Tellingly, the number of statutory definitions is reported to be relatively small across different legal systems.[49] A comprehensive definition according to normative reasons is burdensome and at times counterproductive.

Furthermore, the introduction of new concepts and the redefining of existing ones might interfere with an established classification and thereby lead to confusion. The normative considerations influencing the definition of legal concepts do not necessarily concur with the ontological criteria with which existing classifications are designed. The reason for this is that normative reasons need not be part of the

---

[49] Šarčević, *New approach to legal translation*, 240.

ontological and epistemological reasons underlying the concept's classification.[50] For instance, the reason why all motorised vehicles are called cars has no necessary connection to the question which cars are to be allowed on the highway. Vehicles travelling at under 50 miles an hour might not be allowed to drive on highways and yet still classified as cars – with an engine, moving on four wheels, the typical properties of a car. To be intuitively plausible it is preferable to cover similar phenomena by the same concept, even if their treatment in the law differs.

The choice of legal concepts is thus caught in the tension between two hazards. One occurs if legislators use existing concepts. Then they must accept their ambiguity and cannot define them according to their own normative agenda. The other occurs if they introduce new concepts, or modify existing ones. Then they must undergo the difficult und hazardous process of introducing and redefining them. The more the intension and extension of a legal concept depart from the ones established in ordinary language, the more difficult its application becomes. Therefore, the advantages and disadvantages of new and old concepts must be weighed. Trade-offs have to be made. Normative reasons to realise certain political and moral aims have thus no unrestricted influence on the definition of legal concepts.[51]

3.3 Functional Constraints

Apart from operational constraints, the law's functions might also restrict the influence of normative reasons on legal concepts. This appears at first glance paradoxical. For how can these functions hamper normative reasons if they are themselves normative in kind? The answer lies in one of the essential functions of the law, i.e. to resolve the various political, economic and social conflicts.[52] Therefore legal concepts must be designed for this very purpose. Not all concepts are suitable for it. They must meet several requirements.

First of all, they must be easily communicable. It does not suffice that a few legal experts can understand and administer them. For legal rules, like the constitution or the civil code, regulate the behaviour of virtually every citizen. This would be untenable if only a minority was capable of grasping the legal concepts and the rules with which they are employed. For then only this minority would be able to apply them and adjust their behaviour accordingly. However if the rule of law is to govern, legal concepts must be designed in a way that is understandable to all the people concerned.[53] In this regard, there is a striking difference between scientific and legal concepts. The former helps to 'systematise the data of our experience'.[54]

---

[50] Füßer, *Farewell to 'Legal Positivism'*, 140.

[51] For tradeoffs in the formation of concepts see Gerring, *What Makes a Concept Good* .

[52] J. Waldron, *Law and Disagreement* (Oxford 1998) 147; S. Besson, *The Morality of Conflict* (Oxford 2005) 205.

[53] Bix, *Theories of Meaning and Reference*, 290, argues that the value of 'notice/rule of law' can clash with the lawmaker's intention.

[54] Hempel, *Fundamentals of Concept Formation*, 21.

If this experience is not describable by other means, they might acquire an 'esoteric' character.[55] In contrast, legal concepts do primarily not serve such a descriptive and taxonomic function. They are part of the rules that shall regulate behaviour and solve the mentioned conflicts. If they take on an 'esoteric character' they will lose this capacity, even if they best reflect the normative considerations decisive for the law.

Apart from that, the better legal concepts are communicable, the more the law is open for change. Democratic initiatives are more likely if the public can understand the law and its concepts. Otherwise it would not know whether the law has something worth changing. The more technical legal concepts become the more the democratic character of the law is endangered. If one wished to shape legal concepts according to one's ideological commitments, one must, at the very least, make sure that they are easily communicable.

The communicability of legal concepts has repercussions not only for the choice of concepts but also for their definition. Different people must be able to administer them uniformly. Therefore, legal definitions should not be excessively complex. Their main purpose is not to describe a state of affairs, but to regulate behaviour. For instance, the legal definition of art is primarily not intended to characterise what art is. Therefore, the law need not refer to the theories of philosophy of art to establish what shall be considered as art. Its purpose is to regulate what actions are to be protected. Therefore, a clear and intuitively plausible classification of art everyone can go by could be better than an elaborate definition based on aesthetic principles.

Finally, legal concepts should have, as far as possible, a non-partisan character.[56] For if the rules using them are to solve conflicts, they should not be antagonistic. Conceptual schemes therefore must be as non-controversial as possible, provided that they continue to conform to the legal rules and their consequences. The more partisan they are the greater the risk that they alienate the minority and will have to be modified as a result of new social, economic or political developments as soon as the minority becomes the majority. Conversely, the less they are associated with a particular political program or ideology, the more versatile they are for deployment in different context and for integrating political and moral debates within the law. So even if political reasons supported a specific partisan concept, it might be better to use a more neutral one.

3.4 Benefit Constraints

Lastly, it is worthwhile to consider the benefits of concepts influenced by a certain political program or ideology. These benefits are smaller than would first appear. On the one hand, they ensure that the concepts concur with one's normative objectives.

---

[55] Hempel, *Fundamentals of Concept Formation*, 21, stressing that even esoteric concepts are to have a connection to "experiential terms' available in everyday language.'

[56] Cf. J. Raz, 'On the Nature of Rights', *Mind* (1984) 194.

However, these objectives can, most often, be realised by the already established concepts.[57] There is hardly any condition under which legal consequences shall occur and hardly any such consequence that could not be described with the existing concepts.

Moreover, concepts formed according to normative principles are not in themselves guarantees that these principles are upheld. For as the refutation of thesis 1 made clear,[58] concepts alone do not bring about specific results. They can always be negated or modified by operators like 'no', 'except' and the combination with other concepts.[59] No normatively influenced definition of a concept can prevent deviant principles from being formulated or discussed. This holds in particular, if the result of a decision rests on a balancing test. For then the definition of the used concepts can hardly determine the weight of the different factors that must be considered. So the benefits of normative reason's influence on the definition of legal concepts are limited. When weighed against the associated effort and risks the benefits might turn out too small. This is not to say they are unimportant or not worthwhile considering, but it might explain why the influence of political and ideological considerations on the choice and definition of legal concepts is smaller than appears at first glance.

4 Conclusion

Normative reasons can have a considerable influence on both the choice and definition of legal concepts although these concepts, when taken separately, do not bring about any legal consequences. First, they can influence the choice of these concepts. Such choices must be made between old and new concepts, those evaluatively determinate and those evaluatively indeterminate, and between concepts with different ideological backgrounds. Second, normative reasons can affect the content of legal concepts. Finally, normative reasons can influence the process in which legal concepts are chosen and defined.

Despite all this, the influence of normative reasons is constrained in a number of ways. Legal concepts must be expressed in words that abide by the linguistic rules of ordinary language. Therefore, limitation in the formation of words might impact the formation of concepts. Moreover, the more the application of concepts depends on normative evaluations the more burdensome it becomes. For these evaluations rest on a variety of factors that are difficult to discern and balance. Lastly, the benefits of new and redefined concepts are limited. Thus the advantages a new definition, according to certain normative considerations, must be weighed against the risks of misunderstanding and higher application costs brought about by these concepts.

---

[57] Cf. Gerring and Barresi, *Putting Ordinary Language to Work*, 219: 'neologism result from a failure to survey the existing field of terms and definitions adequately.'

[58] Section 2.

[59] See for this phenomenon Sandrini, *Terminology and Knowledge Engineering*, 131; Löbner, *Semantik*, 102.

These constraints cannot prevent normative reasons from shaping legal concepts. There is even no guarantee that the law will use concepts upon which all those concerned can agree. But these constraints create considerable obstacles if one wants to choose and define legal concepts according to certain political programs and ideologies. This might explain why the evolution of the law has led to many evaluatively indeterminate concepts like property, possession, or contract, and why these concepts have been used by different political regimes. Every conscious attempt to redefine them must bear in mind the risks this induces. Such a reason has a normative status as well. Hence normative reasons themselves might restrain the influence they have on the formation of legal concepts.

The Hand of Midas: When Concepts Turn Legal, or Deflating the Hart-Dworkin Debate

Ralf Poscher

What always puzzles lay people when they are confronted with legal documents is that unlike diagnoses of physicians or analysts reports on the stock market, legal texts almost invariably use no technical terms. But despite the familiarity of the language used, lay people still get the impression that they do not really understand the legal texts. What they experience is a well-established fact of linguistics. Different areas of discourse have their own language. And even if different areas of discourse employ the same term, it may well have a different content.

In German criminal law the marks on a beer coaster can turn it into an authorised document subject to forgery,[1] while the common understanding has a far more fanciful image of authorised documents. In legal interpretation the fact that terms might have a different import in law than in everyday life means that the plain meaning of a legal expression is just one aspect of interpretation – an important aspect, to be sure, but still, only one aspect. Often the development of the content of a legal concept takes as its starting point a comparable concept in everyday discourse and, in some instances, might leave it at that. More often, it modifies the everyday concept, so that it fits the special doctrinal exigencies. That is why lay people have their difficulties.

Usually the discrepancy between the more loose everyday understanding of a term and the technical legal meaning is merely amusing. But sometimes it can have quite serious implications. Recently the United Nations sent an international commission to inquire the conflict in Dafur. The commission had to evaluate the crimes committed in the area under international criminal law. International criminal law establishes genocide and crimes against humanity as distinct criminal offences. The commission found that widespread and massive atrocities were committed in Dafur, which constituted crimes against humanity. But because of a lack of intent to extinct an ethnical group the commission could not corroborate that a genocide in the legal sense was committed. This technical legal finding was a major blow for the

R. Poscher (✉)
Ruhr-University Bochum, Bochum, Germany
e-mail: poscher@poscher.eu

[1] RG, 3 *Deutsche Strafrechtszeitung* (1916) 77; T. Fischer *Strafgesetzbuch und Nebengesetze*, 55th edition (München 2008) § 267 Rn 7.

J.C. Hage, D. von der Pfordten (eds.), *Concepts in Law*, Law and Philosophy Library 88,
DOI 10.1007/978-90-481-2982-9_7, © Springer Science+Business Media B.V. 2009

diplomatic and grass root movement efforts to stop the 'genocide' in Dafur.[2] Ignoring the technical legal subtleties, the general public perceived the report as evidence that the situation in Dafur might not be as bad as the call for action suggested, since no 'genocide' was committed. By its critics, the report was considered partly responsible for the international inaction in the conflict.[3]

The technical legal meaning of terms does not only deviate from the looser use of concepts in the general public. The law does not show much more respect for technical elaborations of terms in specialised areas of knowledge either. The development of legal concepts might well draw on comparable concepts in other disciplines where these have already been systematically developed. If a road sign sets a special speed limit in case of fog, the development of the legal concept of fog might draw on a meteorological concept of fog, which describes and defines the notion by appeal to a certain ratio of humidity, temperature and barometric pressure. But it might also modify the meteorological concept by relying on a sight-factor, for the rationale for the special speed limit is the impairment of sight. Even if concepts are systematically developed in other disciplines, the law does not simply adopt them, but has to modify them to fit its specific needs.

1 Concepts and Conceptions

To clarify the relationship between legal and extra-legal concepts terminologically, it may be helpful to draw loosely on the distinction between concepts and conceptions. The distinction was employed by W. B. Gallie to describe 'essentially contested concepts'.[4] Gallie distinguished certain moral and political concepts like 'good', 'right', 'just' or 'democracy' on the ground that even though they seemed to have some shared common meaning, the criteria for their application were contested in ways that could not be resolved. Political philosophers could agree that democracy – one of Gallie's examples – is centred on the aspiration of increased political equality. Despite this agreement, however, the conflict over which forms of government could be regarded as democratic persists.[5] Gallie described this constellation by

---

[2] An in depth cultural analysis of the discrepancy in the different understandings of 'genocide' is S. Wastell, *How Do We Know a Genocide When We See It? Re-thinking the Most Freighted of Terms Inside and Outside of the Law*, manuscript, forthcoming.

[3] D. Luban, 'Calling Genocide by Its Rightful Name', 7 *Chicago Journal of International Law* (2006–2007) 304.

[4] W.B. Gallie, 'Essentially Contested Concepts' 56 *Proceedings of the Aristotellian Society* (1956) 167. The distinction was taken up by J. Rawls, *A Theory of Justice*, 2nd edition (Cambridge 1999) 5, passim, and R. Dworkin, '*Law's Empire*' (Cambridge 1986) 70–72. For a brief discussion of the distinction, see L.B. Solum, '*Legal Theory Lexicon* 028: Concepts and Conceptions' at *http://lsolum.typepad.com/legal_theory_lexicon/2004/03/legal_theory_le_1.html*. For a more formal discussion see M. Ezcurdia, 'The Concept-Conception Distinction' *Philosophical Issues*, 9, Concepts. (1998), 187–192.

[5] Gallie, *Essentially Contested Concepts*, 184–185.

employing[6] – though not systematically endorsing – the distinction between concept and conception: In political theory different, ultimately non commensurable *conceptions* for the *concept* of 'democracy' are put forward, which make the concept essentially contested.

Though Gallie employed the distinction with an eye to the dispute over concepts in one field of inquiry, namely moral and political philosophy, it can also be employed in describing similar phenomena across different areas of inquiry even if the different conceptions do not make the concept an essentially contested one in Gallie's sense. It holds also for profane concepts employed in different areas of inquiry; they can have a partly shared meaning in the sense that they apply in part to the same entities, but are supported by – in some instances only slightly – different conceptions.

Still more precise would be an account that employs the three-fold distinction among a term, its extension, and its intension.[7] One term can share the core of its extensions across different fields, while having slightly or even radically differing intensions. Owing to the common core of the extension, it is justified to consider such a term ranging across fields as referring to the same concept in the sense of the two-fold distinction between concepts and conceptions. The term 'fog' shares its core extensions in meteorological and legal discourse while having a distinct intension in each. This is different in the case of homonyms, where the same term not only has different intensions but also no shared extensions.[8] In financial and geographical contexts the term 'bank' has an altogether distinct intension in each field and also no shared extensions. In the following the distinction between concepts and conceptions will be applied in this way. I will speak of a *shared concept* if a term, employed in different areas of discourse, shares a core of extensions but might well have distinct intensions. The latter shall be referred to as distinct conceptions.

2 Shared Concepts

It is easy to see that the law employs concepts that are used in everyday or technical contexts, and the law in at least some instances develops conceptions for these concepts that deviate from their everyday or technical counterparts. It can even happen that in different contexts within the law, different conceptions for a single concept are developed. In German law, the concept of a human being is explicated differently in criminal law and in private law. In criminal law, a human being begins to exist

---

[6] Gallie, *Essentially Contested Concepts*, 176.

[7] The distinction is widely used in modern logical semantics. Cf. K. Lorenz, 'Semantik, logische' in J. Mittelstraß (ed.), *Enzyklopädie Philosophie und Wissenschaftstheorie*, vol. 3 (Stuttgart 2004) 776–778, picking up the distinction between 'Bedeutung' (meaning) and 'Sinn' of G. Frege, 'Über Sinn und Bedeutung' in *Zeitschrift für Philosophie und philosophische Kritik* (1892), 25–50.

[8] See G. Pethö, 'What is Polysemy? A Survey of Current Research and Results' in: E.T. Németh and K. Bibok, Károly (eds.), *Pragmatics and the Flexibility of Word Meaning* (Amsterdam 2001) 178, 181–182.

only after a certain point in the process of being born,[9] while in civil law, its existence is already recognised at a certain point after insemination.[10] Both conceptions draw on medical and biological conceptions of human life. The difference in the criminal law and the private law conceptions of human being is not owed to the fact that the criminal law and private law follow different medical or biological conceptions. Rather the difference is explained by means of different systematic exigencies of the criminal law and the private law statutes. In contrast to German private law, German criminal law contains norms especially designed to protect the embryo during pregnancy.[11] To adopt the private law conception in criminal law would defy the criminal laws on abortion. They would be redundant if the embryo were already protected by the general laws on manslaughter. The development of legal conceptions is driven not by medical or biological concerns, but by specific legal and doctrinal exigencies – as in this case, by a systematic profile of the different criminal laws protecting human life.

This is not to say that the law does not take the conceptions of other disciplines in account. By way of developed conceptions, concepts serve as storage places for knowledge, and the law generally tries to develop its conceptions in a way that is reasonably responsive to knowledge reflected in the conceptions of everyday life and specialised disciplines. In taking them into account it will try to stay synchronised with, for example, the sciences. It will seek not to develop a conception of a human being that contradicts consolidated medical or biological knowledge. The reason for the responsiveness of the law to other conceptions is not only informative in nature but also functional: to function well, the law cannot be altogether out of step with the knowledge in the society it is supposed to govern. These functional considerations however, are only negative, general, and gradual. The law can always modify scientific conceptions, even if they are consolidated; it can even adhere to conceptions that have been overcome by scientific knowledge in some instances. The functional exigencies of the law affect the empirical conditions of its efficacy, not its normative validity.

3 The Midas Quality of the Law

That the law develops its own conceptions of concepts shared with other disciplines is ubiquitous. The accommodation of the doctrinal exigencies of the law leads to legal conceptions that at least modify the conceptions used in other fields.

---

[9] BGHSt 10, 291/293; 13, 21/24; 31, 348/352. See A. Eser, 'Vorbemerkungen zu den § 211ff.' in A. Schönke and H. Schröder (eds.), *Strafgesetzbuch*, 27th edition (München 2006) 13 and K. Kühl, 'Vorbemerkung § 211' in: K. Lackner and K. Kühl (eds.), *Strafgesetzbuch*, 26th edition (München 2007) 3.

[10] BGH 25 *Neue juristische Wochenschrift* (1972) 1126; H.G. Bamberger, 'Commentary to § 1', in: H.G. Bamberger and H. Roth (eds.), *Kommentar zum Bürgerlichen Gesetzbuch* Band I, 2nd edition (München 2007) 13; J. Ellenberger and H. Heinrichs, 'Commentary to § 1' in: O. Palandt, *Bürgerliches Gesetzbuch*, 67th edition (München 2008) 7.

[11] §§ 218–219b of the German Criminal Code (StGB).

Linguistically, this leads to polysemy, or at least to a variation in meaning.[12] Polysemy and variations in meaning are largely due to usage in different specialised discourses, where the meaning of terms becomes specific and thus modified. Polysemisation in this sense is what happens to concepts taken up in the law. Philosophically, this linguistic phenomenon accords with pragmatic theories of language, which rely on the use of terms.[13] In the perspective of such theories, it comes as no surprise that terms acquire a related but different meaning in different areas of practice. Different practices, such as law and medicine, generate different meanings. The pragmatic exigencies of a practice determine the meaning, and they are different in the law on the one hand and in medicine or biology on the other.

In a qualified sense the specificity of legal conceptions is not only ubiquitous, but pervasive. Even if the development of a legal conception were to lead to the same conception as in the area of discourse that the law is drawing upon, this would not deprive the legal conception of its legal specificity. First, it would be specific to the law in the sense that it could only be taken up there, for it complies with the specific exigencies of the law, not just because it is scientifically convincing. Second, after being taken up it would still stand under different conditions of usage, as would become apparent in the case of a change in the legal material. If there had only been laws on murder and manslaughter, the criminal legal conception of a human being might have adopted a certain medical definition that included a foetus to protect the unborn life. If the legislator were to introduce laws on abortion, this would necessarily affect the criminal conception, but would not affect the medical or biological counterpart.

Law is like King Midas in the ancient legend. King Midas hosted the former foster and schoolmaster of Dionysus, the satyr Silenos, when he lost his way after drinking too much wine. Midas hosted Silenos for 10 days. On the eleventh day, he brought him back to Dionysus. In gratitude Dionysus granted King Midas the fulfilment of a wish. Midas wished that everything he touched would turn to gold. And so it happened: whatever Midas touched with his hand turned into gold.[14] Just as whatever Midas touched turned into gold, any concept taken up by the law turns into a legal concept, in the sense that a conception specific to the law has to be adopted.[15] The law can only develop its conceptions with respect to those specific

---

[12] What is considered as polysemy depends on how strongly two meanings have to differ, to be considered different and not just variations. The boundary is drawn differently by different linguistic approaches. See Pethö, *What is Polysemy?* 178. Polysemy shall be employed in the following in a liberal or even loose sense that also covers variations due to specialisation.

[13] For a brief account of theories of use W.G. Lycan, *Philosophy of Language – A contemporary introduction* (London/New York 2000) 88–99. For a contemporary elaboration, see P. Horwich, *Meaning* (Oxford 1998).

[14] P. Ovidius Naso, *Metamorphosen*, transl. M. V. Albrecht, (Stuttgart 1994) 568–573; R. V. Ranke-Graves, *Griechische Mythologie*, 12th edition (Reinbek bei Hamburg 1999) 255–258.

[15] Already Kelsen employed the Midas legend. In one context to illustrate his thesis of the identity of state and law (everything the state touches becomes law), H. Kelsen, *Allgemeine Staatslehre*, (Berlin 1925) 44, and H. Kelsen, 'Justiz und Verwaltung' 1–2 Zeitschrift für soziales Recht (1928–1930) 81. On another occasion to explain the retroactive annulation of norms, which legally presupposes the existence of the norm: 'Just as everything Midas touched turned into gold, everything

methods, doctrinal standards, specific values, and institutional settings of the legal system in which the conception has to be applied.

4 Legal and Moral Conceptions

Legal philosophers have worried little about relations between and among legal and meteorological, biological, and medical concepts. The specialization of concepts that the law shares with other areas of discourse is widely recognised. There may be mockery of legal language as legalese with its distortion of everyday meanings, but there are generally no theoretical debates. Even in the sciences, however, there are exceptions to its generally unexciting relationship to the law. A nice example is the recently rediscovered case of James Maurice v. Samuel Judd.[16] Early in the nineteenth century in New York there were complaints in connection with the purchase of fish oil. Especially in barrels of liver oil, large portions of fish water were found underneath the oil. In 1817, initiated by the leather industry, which suffered from the impure oil, New York State passed a statute requiring inspections for 'fish oil' barrels.[17] Mr. Judd, a candle maker and oil merchant, objected to the inspections of three barrels of whale oil in his stock on the ground that whales were mammals and the statute required inspection only for oils from fish. The ensuing trial over Judd's sale of uninspected whale oil drew enormous public attention, for it was perceived as emblematic of how the sciences were taking over the common ways in which people represented their world in theological, mythological and traditional categories – and in all of these whales were considered fish.[18] For a Midas-account of the law, the judgment came as no surprise. After hearing numerous expert witnesses from the sciences, from whalers, oil merchants, and the leather industry, the jury decided that for the law whales remained fish, despite the scientific evidence and classifications of the scientific experts.[19]

The theoretical arousal of Maurice v. Judd over laws relation to the sciences was of rather episodical nature. In this it is very different from the one relation legal theory is persistently concerned about: the relation between legal and moral concepts. In a broader sense, the relation between law and morality has been the central focus

---

to which the law refers becomes law, i.e., something legally existing', H. Kelsen, *General Theory of Law and State* (Harvard 1945) 161. The second use of the Midas legend is often brought in connection with Kelsen's claim that 'it is ... possible for the legal order, by obliging ... to respect or apply certain moral norms or political principles or opinions of experts, to transform these norms, principles or opinions into legal norms', ibid, 132. Cf. for instance L. Green, 'Positivsm', in: E.N. Zalta (ed.), *The Stanford Encyclopedia of Philosophy* (Spring 2003 Edition), URL: http://plato.stanford.edu/archives/spr2003/entries/legal-positivism/ For the difference between the incorporation by reference Kelsen is concerned about and the phenomenon of shared concepts, see infra at note 42.

16 D. Graham Burnett, *Trying Leviathan* (Princeton 2007).

17 Burnett, *Trying Leviathan*, 151–153.

18 Burnett, *Trying Leviathan*, 4–5.

19 Burnett, *Trying Leviathan*, 178.

of legal philosophy more or less from its beginnings. Since the middle of the last century it has taken the form of a debate over positivism, which has preoccupied and dominated Anglo-American legal theory ever since. But the general account for shared concepts holds for the law and morality, just as it holds for the law and meteorology, the law and medicine, the law and biology, and so on. The relation between legal and moral concepts is special only in so far as very central concepts of the law, such as equality, freedom, and dignity, to name only a few, are also central concepts in moral discourse. But this centrality shared in both fields does not affect the general polysemic mechanism described above. Moral concepts, like any other concepts, are spelled out as genuine legal conceptions when they are introduced to the law.

A similar point was made by Hermann Kantorowicz. In his *The definition of Law*, he devoted a whole chapter to the defence of the distinction between law and morality against the argument that many legal prohibitions simply reduplicate their moral counterparts. One of his replies to the reduplication thesis evoked briefly the ubiquity of the phenomena that law shares rules with other disciplines:

> If this were so, even rules of the multiplication table would become legal if embodied in, let us say, an Act of Parliament containing tariff of taxes.[20]

His main argument for the distinction between law and morality relied on the Kantian distinction between internally and externally binding norms: morality addresses the internal attitude towards an action, while law just addresses factual behaviour. From this it follows that moral obligations which are transformed into legal obligations change their character in the course of the transformation.

> Here an ethico-religious rule has become legal; at the price, however, of losing its characteristic internality.[21]

His point about the transformation of moral rules into legal rules, though focused on the internal-external-distinction, is similar to the one about the shared concepts. They can only go legal at the price of changing their content.

Even closer to the 'Midas' reading of the law is Max Weber's observation on the relation between concepts in law and social science, examining the phenomenon from the other direction. In his methodological writings he was concerned to establish the uniqueness of social sciences compared to natural sciences, but also compared to the law. At the level of concepts he was confronted with the fact that many of the concepts employed in the social sciences had been imported from the law. As he observed in his *Critique of Stammler*, the sharing of concepts was one of the factors leading to methodological confusions that fail to respect the distinctiveness of social sciences and the law.

> On the other hand ... important branches of the empirical sociocultural sciences, especially political sciences and economic disciplines, employ legal concepts for terminological purposes. ... They also employ these concepts for the purpose of what might be called a

[20] H. Kantorowicz, *The Definition of Law* (Cambridge, UK 1958; 1st edition 1939) 45.
[21] Kantorowicz, *The Definition of Law*, 45.

> *preliminary* analysis of their own subject matter. ... This use of legal concepts is chiefly due to the advanced state of the development of legal thought. Therefore it is always necessary to keep the following point clearly in mind. Suppose that a political or economical inquiry undertakes to conceive its subject matter in terms of the 'problematic' of politics or economics. In that case, legal concepts acquire a facticity that necessarily changes their meaning. Whenever this happens, the inquiry is no longer at the level on which preliminary analysis is undertaken by employing legal concepts.[22]

The change of meaning that Weber observed on the side of the social sciences implies by logic a distinctive meaning on the side of the law; by analogy, it implies the same relation between law and morality. The legal conceptions differ from their social sciences or moral counterparts even if they employ the same concept and even if they have used them for a 'preliminary analysis'.

Recently Danny Priel adduced a similar argument in the debate over inclusive and exclusive positivism. Priel holds the view,

> that in all ... instances in which moral words are mentioned in the law, the reference is to a legal concept, which often bears a close relationship to the moral concept ... but is logically independent of it.[23]

He supports this view with a meta-ethical and an epistemological argument. The common ground in the inclusive-exclusive-debate is that it is at least conceivable that the law requires concepts shared in law and morality to be interpreted 'in the light of the best moral understanding'[24] of the concept.[25] Yet, Priel argues, the history of moral philosophy has shown that there is either no best moral concept at all or that at any rate we have no way of knowing it:

> I think there are good reasons for thinking that the view that we might ever discover or know the 'best' or 'correct' morality is mistaken.[26]

Priel argues that if there is no such thing, or at least no knowledge of such thing, as the 'best moral understanding', the legal concept cannot be the same as the 'best moral' concept, but has to be specific to law. And even if the best moral understanding were known today – so Priel's argument – it would not render past legal decisions, where no such knowledge was at hand, illegal. Even if we knew today as a moral truth that the death penalty constitutes a cruel and unusual punishment, past judgments to the contrary would still have to be considered legal, at least from a positivist standpoint:

> At the time the judge handed down his judgment, to the best of everyone's knowledge the judge was acting as the law, including its prohibition on cruel and unusual punishment as then understood by the legal community, required ... I think positivists are committed to the

[22] M. Weber, *Critique of Stammler*, transl. by Guy Oakes (New York 1977; original 1907) 136.
[23] D. Priel, 'Farewell to the Exclusive – Inclusive Debate' 25 *Oxford Journal of Legal Studies* (2005), 682.
[24] Cf. J. Raz, 'Dworkin: A New Link in the Chain' 74 *California Law Review* (1986), 1110.
[25] Priel, *Farewell to the Exclusive – Inclusive Debate*.
[26] Ibid.

> view that the content of the law of a community is in some way fixed by what the majority of the legal community thinks it is. If it were otherwise, it could be that an entire legal community can get the law wrong.[27]

This shows, in Priel's view, that – at least for positivists – a specific legal concept of 'cruel and unusual' would have to be acknowledged even if we know the moral truth. Contrary to Priel, however, the specificity of legal conceptions for concepts shared with moral or political philosophy neither depends on metaethics or epistemology, nor does it hold for positivists alone. It is not a lack of objective moral truth or its epistemic status that accounts for the development of distinctly legal conceptions. Rather, that development is owing to the legal method and the doctrinal and institutional exigencies of law that are peculiar to it.

In developing legal conceptions of liberty, equality, dignity and the like, the law can inform itself about similar conceptions in moral or political philosophy in the sense of Weber's 'preliminary analysis'. It does so just as it informs itself in a preliminary way about meteorology, medicine, and biology. Whatever insights such a consideration of conceptions in other areas of discourse might bring about, these insights will always have to be built into a specific legal conception that takes into account the specific legal history, methodology, forms of argumentation and institutional setting of the law.[28] For example, whatever the answer to the moral question of torture in ticking-bomb scenarios might be, the development of a legal conception of human dignity for a constitution in which it is protected[29] has to take into account the institutional conditions that accompany a legal power to use torture within public security services. It has to take into account the fact that a legal conception of human dignity allowing torture is not without specific costs that are due to the institutional settings in which the legal conception, as opposed to the moral conception, has to operate. One thinks here of the inflationary tendency of a legal authorization of torture for which there is empirical evidence[30] stemming from the legal handling of factual errors, rules about administrative discretion, and executive prerogatives. Thus, there are reasons peculiar to the legal system speaking in favour of a conception of human dignity that would lead to an absolute protection against

---

[27] Ibid.

[28] For a more detailed account of the particularities of the legal framework R. Poscher, 'Rechtsprechung und Verfassungsrecht' in: W. Erbguth and J. Masing (eds.), *Die Bedeutung der Rechtsprechung im System der Rechtsquellen: Europarecht und nationales Recht* (Stuttgart 2005) 127, 132–145. For an account reflecting the division of power, see R. Poscher, 'Funktionenordnung des Grundgesetzes' in: W. Hoffmann-Riem, E. Schmidt-Aßmann and A. Voßkuhle (eds.), *Grundlagen des Verwaltungsrechts*, Band I, Methoden, Maßstäbe, Aufgaben, Organisation (München 2006) § 8 Sec. 51–64.

[29] As in the German case in Art. 1 Sec. 1: 'Human dignity shall be inviolable. To respect and protect it shall be the duty of all state authority.'

[30] For the experience in Israel see A. Imseis, 'Moderate Torture On Trial: Critical Reflections on the Israeli Supreme Court Judgment Concerning the Legality of General Security Service Interrogation Methods' 19 *Berkeley Journal of International Law* (2001) 328, 339–349.

torture. These specific reasons have to be considered for the legal conception, not for the moral conception, and could yield differing conceptions as a consequence.[31]

Other examples can easily be added: For the question of whether capital punishment is a violation of human dignity, the legal conception has to take into account if – as in Germany – the constitution has a special article banning capital punishment[32] – a fact that has no bearing on the moral discourse. The difference between the internal aspect of morality and the external aspect of law, the difference that Kantorowicz insisted upon, has played itself out in the German adjudication on abortion. Even if from a certain moral standpoint – say, the Roman Catholic standpoint – abortion could not be justified, its legal regulation has to take into account empirical data suggesting that a better protection of the unborn life is achieved by means of a regulation that does not force women into illegality and provides for a possibility of widespread professional support and counsel.[33] These specifics of the legal as opposed to the moral regulation of abortion have to be factored into the legal conceptions of human life and dignity. It is not only in legal systems with a case law tradition that a legal concept of *liberty* has to take into account the past decisions of higher courts along with the legal history of fundamental rights within its tradition in order to develop a specific legal conception of liberty. It might draw on the positive versus negative debate on liberty in political philosophy,[34] but it cannot simply hand over the legal concept to the philosophers.[35]

The linguistic fact that the law develops its own conceptions of concepts it shares with other disciplines has a deep and profound cause in the structure of the institutional and doctrinal practice of law, which develops methods, doctrinal standards, and institutions that set the parameters for legal conceptions. These parameters are distinct not only from the parameters in the sciences, but also from the parameters in morality and politics. The argument for the distinctiveness of legal conceptions is not linguistic in character. The colloquial fact of polysemy and meaning variation is only the consequence of the specificity of doctrinal legal practice. The comparison with other disciplines where the insight that the law develops and has to develop its own conceptions according to its own doctrinal needs seems humdrum, making merely apparent what holds, too, for the relation of the law to morality, but tends to be overlooked owing to the seriousness and centrality of the material questions involved. The difference between the relation of the law to moral philosophy on the one hand and other disciplines on the other is not structural but quantitative and qualitative. Quantitatively many, though not all, legal questions have an equivalent

---

[31] R. Poscher, 'Menschenwürde als Tabu. Die verdeckte Rationalität eines absoluten Rechtsverbots der Folter' in: G. Beestermöller and H. Brunkhorst (eds.), *Rückkehr der Folter* (München 2006) 75–87; R. Poscher 'Menschenwürde im Staatsnotstand' in P. Bahr and M. Heinig (eds.), *Menschenwürde in der säkularen Verfassungsordnung* (Tübingen 2006) 215–231.

[32] Art. 102: 'Capital punishment is abolished.'

[33] BVerfGE 88, 203f.

[34] For example I. Berlin, *Two concepts of liberty* (Oxford 1959).

[35] Cf. R. Poscher, *Grundrechte als Abwehrrechte. Reflexive Ordnung rechtlich geordneter Freiheit* (Tübingen 2003) 109–143.

in moral or political theory; qualitatively the two disciplines for one thing share some of their most important and crucial concepts, not only profane ones as in the case of meteorology; for another they are both normative disciplines. So there are good reasons for the fact that the law is far more interested in moral and political theory than in meteorology. But the interest is an interest in Weber's sense, namely of a 'preliminary analysis'. Sharing concepts with other disciplines does not liberate law from the task of developing its own conceptions.

5 Consequences for Jurisprudence

What is the jurisprudential importance of the superficially humdrum but at a deeper level crucial, insight that the law has to develop its own conceptions of shared concepts? Priel uses the genuinely legal quality of legal conceptions to call into question the inclusive-exclusive debate within positivism.[36] And even though his argument from metaethics and epistemology to support the specificity of legal conceptions is beside the far more general and important point that legal methods and the doctrinal and institutional exigencies of the law are responsible for its Midas quality, he is correct in the conclusion he draws. Both inclusive as well as exclusive positivists share the assumption that moral concepts are of significance to the law. The point at which they differ is whether moral concepts can be integrated into the law. Inclusive positivists believe that law can integrate moral concepts by referring to them, thereby establishing the legal pedigree essential to the positivist concept of law.[37] By contrast exclusive positivists do not think that moral concepts can become a part of the law. The most prominent account of this latter position, by Joseph Raz, relies on an argument from authority.[38] In referring to moral concepts, the law would be handing over its claim of authority, understood as giving an independent reason for action, to morality. In the case in which the law refers to moral concepts it is thus not the law but morality that provides the reason for action and exercises authority. Since the claim of authority is an essential element of the law, moral concepts cannot become part of the law.

If, however, concepts that the law shares with morality are not introduced into the law with their moral conceptions but with distinctly legal conceptions, the inclusive-exclusive debate loses its point.[39] Both sides of the debate are, then, mistaken. On the one hand the law does not integrate moral conceptions into the law, as the

---

[36] Priel, *Farewell to the Exclusive – Inclusive Debate.*
[37] K.E. Himma, 'Inclusive Legal Positivism', in: J. Coleman and S. Shapiro (eds.), *Oxford Handbook of Jurisprudence and Philosophy of Law* (Oxford 2001) 125.
[38] J. Raz, 'Legal Positivism and the Sources of Law', in: *The Authority of Law: Essays on Law and Morality* (Oxford 1979) 37–52; J. Raz, 'Authority, Law, and Morality', in: *Ethics in the Public Domain: Essays in the Morality of Law and Politics* (Oxford 1994) 210–237. For an overview of the exclusive position see A. Marmor, 'Exclusive Legal Positivism' in Coleman and Shapiro, *Oxford Handbook of Jurisprudence and Philosophy of Law*, 104–124.
[39] Priel, *Farewell to the Exclusive – Inclusive Debate.*

inclusive positivists would have us believe. The law only employs concepts that it shares with morality. It might, in the sense of Weber's preliminary analysis, further draw on moral conceptions for those concepts, but only as a means of developing specific legal conceptions. Only these legal conceptions become part of the law.

On the other hand, the law does not hand over its authority to morality, for the independent reasons it gives for action do not rely on moral conceptions but on specific legal conceptions of concepts that the law shares with morality.[40] The problem of authority might arise when the law incorporates norms by reference in the technical sense, like in conflict of law rules, where the law refers to the rules of a foreign legal order.[41] But first, the technical incorporation of norms by reference is not what happens when the law develops conceptions of concepts it shares with morality; and second, technical incorporations by reference are not the incidents that have sparked the internal-external debate. The internal-external debate arose out of the fact that the law employs – prominently in its fundamental rights guarantees but also in its other statutes, precedents and argumentations – concepts like liberty, dignity, fairness and the like, which are also used in the moral discourse. The debate did not arise around regulations which technically incorporated a special moral codex by reference, for example a codex of the Vatican, and it would be a misconception of the concepts the law shares with morality to understand them in such a way. Reference by incorporation is a very limited special case in law, which is also doctrinally identified as a very limited special case.[42] It should not be confounded with the question of concepts law shares with morality.[43]

But the insight into the specificity of legal conceptions has consequences well beyond positivism.[44] The entire Hart-Dworkin-debate, with which the Anglo-American jurisprudence has been preoccupied for almost 40 years now,[45]

---

[40] For a similar argument see T. Sebok, *Legal Positivism in American Jurisprudence* (Cambridge 1998) 307–312, with the idea that the complex rules of recognition do not lead to their moral elements playing out as in a purely moral judgment.

[41] Even in cases of incorporation by reference, the authority-question might have to be answered differently for different kinds of incorporations: static incorporations, which are mostly regarded merely as an editorial matter, or dynamic or ambulatory incorporations, which also incorporate future changes.

[42] J.M. Kayes, 'Incorporation by Reference in Legislation' 25 *Statute Law Review* (2004), 180–195.

[43] See for example Green, *Positivsm*, who does neither differentiate between incorporation and the phenomenon of shared concepts, nor between different forms of incorporation, nor between norms incorporated into the law and norms used in the formulation of the law, i.e. grammatical standards.

[44] Contrary to Priel, *Farewell to the Exclusive – Inclusive Debate*, the argument from the specificity of legal conceptions does not depend on premises genuine to positivist.

[45] H.L.A. Hart, *The Concept of Law* (Oxford 1961), R. Dworkin, *Taking Rights Seriously* (Cambridge US 1977); H.L.A. Hart, 'Postscript' in: *The Concept of Law,* 2nd ed. (Oxford 1994) 238–276; R. Dworkin 'Hart's Postscript and the Character of Political Philosophy' 24 *Oxford Journal of Legal Studies* (2004), 1. The sentiment that the debate is outworn is widely spread: J. Waldron, 'Legal and Political Philosophy' in Coleman and Shapiro, *Oxford Handbook of Jurisprudence and Philosophy of Law*, 381: 'flat and repetitive'. More judgments along these line at B. Tamanaha, 'The Contemporary Relevance of Legal Positivism', 32 *Australian Journal of Legal*

rests at least to a large degree on Dworkin's attack on Hart with the idea that in hard cases the law has to draw on moral principles of liberty, equality, dignity and alike and that he could show that this is what courts actually do.[46] Dworkin's argument challenged at least two central tenets of positivism: First, it established a connection between law and morality that called the positivist's separation thesis[47] into question. If the law needs to resort to moral principles to adjudicate hard cases, there seems to be a necessary connection between the law and morality, which positivists of course deny.[48]

Second, it challenged Hart's model of adjudication[49]: According to the positivist model of adjudication, morality or politics comes into play when the legal material in a case does not provide a clear answer to a legal question. In hard cases, judges, lawyers, and legal scholars are no longer practicing law; rather they are taking refuge in moral or political decisions. Thus, there is a place for moral or political theory in the positivist model of adjudication, but only, so to speak, beyond the law, when the legal reasons have been exhausted and no decision can be reached on legal grounds. Dworkin wanted to show that this model is wrong, for, he argued, judges and lawyers understand their debates in hard cases involving such concepts as liberty, equality and dignity as legal debates.[50] It was only to accommodate Dworkin's critique and the legal practice that Dworkin referred to, that positivism – and, indeed, Hart himself[51] – endorsed 'inclusive positivism' as the idea that the law can explicitly or implicitly bring certain moral standards into the law.

But if law is like King Midas, then the entire debate rests upon a common error and deflates. The law and morality only share common concepts but not common conceptions. It is the very task of the law, or more precisely, of everyone working within the doctrinal framework of the law – judges, lawyers, doctrinal scholars and so on – to work out genuine legal conceptions by observing the methods that are true to the law, that respect the history of the given legal tradition, and that take into account the specific institutional settings of the law. To draw on moral reasoning in this process neither leads to morality's becoming part of the law, nor does it make the relation between the law and morality structurally unique by comparison with its relation to other disciplines. The law draws on moral conceptions as it draws on meteorology, medicine, or biology – without any need to trigger philosophically

---

Philosophy (2007) 2, 36–37 and B. Leiter, 'Beyond the Hart/Dworkin Debate: The Methodology Problem in Jurisprudence' 48 *American Journal of Jurisprudence* (2003) 17.

[46] Dworkin, *Taking Rights Seriously*, 22–31.

[47] For the variety of aspects of the separation thesis see L. Green, 'Positivism and the Inseparability of Law and Morals' 83 *NYU Law Review* (2008), forthcoming. The aspect referred to here is the separation of the law and morality in the dimension of validity. In so far the separation thesis holds that there is no necessary connection between the validity of a legal rule and its conformity to morality.

[48] Ibid.

[49] Hart, *The Concept of Law*, 173–204.

[50] For the argument from dissent, Dworkin, *Law's Empire*, see T. Endicott, 'Are there any Rules?' 5 *The Journal of Ethics* (2001) 199, 209–211.

[51] Hart, *The Concept of Law*, 250–254.

intense debates about the law being necessarily meteorological, or law having incorporated biology.

Just as the law's relation to the sciences, the relation to morality is, however, not only informative but also to a certain degree functional. As the law can only estrange itself to a certain degree from the scientific knowledge stored in acknowledged scientific conceptions, it can only estrange itself from the moral conceptions of its society to a certain degree without thereby running the risk of affecting the conditions of its empirical effectiveness. But these functional considerations are only general, and gradual. The law can always modify moral conceptions, even if they are widely shared. As for its relation to the sciences, the functional relation holds only on a general level and, as in the case of the sciences, it is not a relation that affects the normative dimension of validity, but only the empirical dimension of the law's efficacy. The loose functional relation that the law bears with other fields of knowledge does not establish a normatively necessary connection between the law and morality that would challenge the separation thesis as a claim of independent validity conditions. The relationship between law and morality is structurally comparable to the relation between morality and other disciplines, such as architectural statics. Sacral buildings may become socially dysfunctional if they violate religious laws. A mosque not facing Mecca might not be accepted by a Muslim community, but it will not collapse. Structurally the functional relationship between the law and morality is not different from the relationship between architecture and religion. There may be functional relations, but they are not constitutive.

For his argument Dworkin relied on the actual legal practice. In certain theoretical exaggerations of Dworkin's argument with which positivists intend to test the theoretical viability of their positions, fictional legal systems are construed which consist only of one rule, for example, 'Do what is just.'[52] But even in such a case, in a developed legal system the concept of 'just' would have to be spelled out into a legal conception, which takes the specific exigencies of the legal institutions, the legal history, precedence, methods, and the like into account, all of which are different for morality. Historically the development of the law as a distinct social practice has been a gradual process. This process included the development of a specific set of institutions, but also the development of a specific system of doctrinal legal meaning[53] [54], both of which are related to each other and had to grow out of undifferentiated religious, moral, political and economical practices. In this process of social differentiation law acquired not only an autonomy of its institutions, but also an autonomy of the legal system of meaning that gives orientation for the

[52] Cf. Tamanaha, *The Contemporary Relevance of Legal Positivism*, 31.

[53] For the Roman law, see B. Frier, *The Rise of the Roman Jurists* (Princeton 1985) 184–196, who describes how a specific legal thinking slowly started to established itself in the first century B.C. within the Roman institutions.

[54] For the distinction between law as a doctrinal system meaning and a system of social action, which receives its identity from its orientation at the doctrinal system of meaning, see Weber, *Critique of Stammler*, 112.

social action in and around the institutions of the law.[55] At least in developed legal systems, as the ones western civilisations have brought about, the complexity of the institutions and the legal material these institutions have produced have reached a level at which the Midas touch of the law becomes pervasive. Even though the Midas quality of the law is contingent in the long historical perspective of social differentiation, it is a defining feature of developed legal systems in functionally differentiated societies.

If the King Midas-account of the law is correct, there are two main conclusions to be drawn from the deflation of the Hart-Dworkin debate. First, Dworkin was right in pointing out that in developing some of its conceptions the law draws on moral or political theory. From this it does not, however, follow that the separation thesis of positivism is mistaken. Not in the sense Dworkin suggested, let alone in an even more fundamental way. The law does not necessarily rely on moral conceptions in hard cases, for it has to come up with a specific legal conception in every instance. It would have to develop it if no moral conception were at hand, but it also has to develop it if a moral conception is at hand, for it has, at the very least, to adjust it to the specific exigencies of law. There is a weak relation in so far as the law can consider moral conceptions in the process of developing its own. This, however, is a weak relation, which exists between the law and many other disciplines, too. It does not endanger the separation thesis.

Moreover the sharing of concepts between the law and morality affects neither the sufficiency nor the necessity component of the separation thesis.[56] The sufficiency component of the separation thesis denies that it is sufficient for a norm to be legally valid that it reproduces the content of a moral principle. The denial is not challenged by the sharing of concepts. Moral conceptions or rules are simply used to develop legal conceptions, which are proper to the legal system. They do not become law as such, let alone simply by virtue of coining a moral principle. To speak of the necessity of the separation is to deny that there are moral constraints imposed on the validity of the law. A norm is not invalid simply because it contradicts certain moral standards. That moral conceptions – as meteorological or medical ones – *can* serve as a resource to develop legal conceptions, does not imply that legal conceptions *have to* draw on them. The informational relation between legal and moral conceptions of shared concepts does not imply that the validity of a legal rule depends on its being in accord with the moral conception. Moral conceptions can be sources of information for building their legal counterparts but impose no constraints on the validity of the law. The constraints on the development of legal conceptions derive from legal methods and from the doctrinal and institutional exigencies of the law itself.

---

[55] For a detailed description of the modern law as even an autopoietic system, see N. Luhmann, *Law as a Social System* (Oxford 2004).

[56] A comprehensive account of the distinction applied to the inclusive-exclusive debate is Himma, *Inclusive Legal Positivism*.

Second, the positivist model of adjudication, an element of legal positivism that Hart shares with Hans Kelsen,[57] is flawed.[58] According to the positivist account of adjudication, there is no legal solution to hard cases.[59] In hard cases, judges are considered to be authorised to decide following their own extra legal criteria.[60] If they have to adjudicate vague concepts that are also used in moral or political theory, they have to choose a moral or political standard of their own in order to come to a decision. This model splits the process of adjudication in hard cases into two phases: first, a legal phase, second a non-legal phase in which the judges refer to moral or political standards. Instead, when judges, lawyers, or legal scholars refer to moral or political theory in order to develop legal conceptions of shared concepts they do not shift gears. They do not do law until a case gets hard and then shift gears to a make moral or political decision. There is no boundary of legal discourse that they cross when they decide hard cases. They do not leave the law and become moral philosophers or political theorists when they draw on moral or political theory. They do what is always done in the law. The law takes into account the knowledge of other disciplines and accommodates it to its specific needs. This is what a major part of the hard work on the body of law is all about. Relating to other fields of knowledge is nothing special to the law's relation to moral or political theory, but ubiquitous. The knowledge that the law draws upon is built into the legal conceptions, which have a content, quality, and life of their own.

Dworkin was right to criticise the positivist model of adjudication and he was right to insist on the legal quality of disputes, even in hard cases. He is mistaken, however, in suggesting that this presupposes that moral principles and theories have to be introduced to the law.[61] He ignores the difference between concepts and conceptions he himself helped to establish in political theory. That the law employs concepts which are also discussed in moral theory and that law can inform itself about moral conceptions does not lead to these conceptions becoming law. The

---

[57] H. Kelsen, 'On the Theory of Interpretation', 10 *Legal Studies* (1990) 130 (original version 1934); Kelsen, *Reine Rechtslehre* 242–247, 346–354. On the different phases of Kelsen's approach, see S. Paulson, 'Kelsen on Legal Interpretation', 10 *Legal Studies* (1990), 136.

[58] Hart (*The Concept of Law*, 259) in any case knew about the deficient character of his ideas on adjudication: 'But I certainly wish to confess now that I said far too little in my book about the topic of adjudication and legal reasoning and, in particular, about arguments from what my critics call legal principles. I now agree that it is a defect of this book that principles are touched upon only in passing.' Kelsen's theory of adjudication is widely considered as underdeveloped, too. See Paulson, *Kelsen on Legal Interpretation*, 136f.

[59] That positivism is not bound to this concept of adjudication is a point that J. Gardner, 'Legal Positivism: 5½ Myths', 46 *American Journal of Jurisprudence* (2001), 211–214, rightly insists upon. More accurately one should speak of the theory of adjudication the most prominent figures of positivism have very influentially endorsed.

[60] For an attempt to reactivate this aspect of legal positivism as a theory of normative authorization see M. Jestaedt , 'Rechtsprechung und Rechtsetzung – eine deutsche Perspektive' in Erbguth and Masing, *Die Bedeutung der Rechtsprechung*, 25 and 75–79; M. Jestaedt, *Das mag in der Theorie richtig sein . . . ,* (Tübingen 2006) 43–85.

[61] R. Dworkin, *Freedom's Law* (Oxford 1996) 331, 343.

orientation provided by specifically legal methods, doctrines, and institutions will thus always produce specifically legal conceptions. Like King Midas, law cannot avoid it.

Acknowledgments I thank Dennis Patterson, Brian Tamanaha and Stanley Paulson for their encouraging, critical and always helpful comments on drafts of this article as well as the participants of the special workshop on General Concepts in Law at the XXIII World Congress of Philosophy of Law and Social Philosophy in Cracow for their comments on a talk in which the core idea of this paper was presented. My thanks also go to the members of the Rutgers Law School in Camden and of the Cardozo Law School in New York who attended presentations of the paper for their comments, which pointed at issues I had not sufficiently addressed.

After Conceptual Analysis: The Rise of Practice Theory

Dennis Patterson

General jurisprudence is the study of the most general features of law. The tradition of analytic jurisprudence – one that spans from Hobbes to Coleman – has exhibited a sustained focus on identifying the constitutive features of law. For some time, this question has been framed as the search for the essential or necessary features of the concept of 'law'. But a look at the tradition reveals that this is only one of a number of ways of looking at law from a similar vantage point. That vantage point or perspective focuses on the structure of law. For a variety of reasons, this focus is changing and a new question is emerging.

This essay is written at a time when the field of analytic jurisprudence is in a state of flux. For the last several decades, debate has centred around evaluating and responding to Ronald Dworkin's critiques of positivism. While there are (and no doubt will continue to be) philosophers with an interest in these questions, discussion in the field is moving to other topics. One of these topics is the focus of this essay.

Stated in general terms, my interest lies in explicating the idea of law as a certain sort of practice. The idea of law as a 'practice' is intuitively obvious. Law is an iterative enterprise where practitioners make claims over time in forms that repeat themselves, albeit in sometimes unfamiliar ways. A feature of law's iterative character is that the practice is conducted in concert with others. In a sense, practitioners of law are 'together' in the enterprise. What does it mean to say that law is something we do 'together'?

John Austin's view of the nature of law dominated Anglo-Saxon jurisprudential thinking from the nineteenth to well into the twentieth century. Famously, Austin regarded a law as an order backed by threat of sanction for noncompliance. One important, additional factor was that the threat issued from a 'sovereign'. Taken together, these elements became the so-called 'Command Theory of Law'.

The view met its end in a work that is still regarded as the most important work of legal theory in the Anglo-American tradition, H.L.A. Hart's *The Concept of Law.*[1]

D. Patterson (✉)
Rutgers University School of Law, Camden, US
e-mail: dpatters@camden.rutgers.edu

[1] H.L.A. Hart, *The Concept of Law*, 2nd edition (Oxford 1994; 1st edition 1961).

J.C. Hage, D. von der Pfordten (eds.), *Concepts in Law*, Law and Philosophy Library 88,
DOI 10.1007/978-90-481-2982-9_8, © Springer Science+Business Media B.V. 2009

Hart argued that Austin's account of the nature of law fails because of Austin's failure to successfully marry threats and sovereignty. That is, Hart exposed the weakness in Austin's picture of law when he asked the question whether there was any substantive difference between the order of a gunman and that of a sovereign. Seeing none, Hart concluded that Austin's account of the nature of law failed to tell us what it was about a legal system that made it 'law' and not a normative system of another sort. Having demolished Austin's picture of law, it fell to Hart to replace it with an alternative.

Before describing Hart's accomplishment in *The Concept of Law,* it is necessary to comment on the nature of his project. Hart was deeply attracted to the professional philosophy of his day, especially the approach to philosophy exhibited in the work of J.L. Austin.[2] While Hart had an interest in the work of other philosophers, especially Wittgenstein, Hart was his own man, philosophically. Finally, Hart self-described *The Concept of Law* as, among other things, a work in 'descriptive sociology'.[3] With these disparate elements in view, what was Hart's project?

One way of answering this question is to ask whether Hart was doing 'conceptual analysis'. In the late nineteen fifties, it was quite fashionable philosophically to conceive of philosophy as an armchair exercise devoted to the search for the necessary and sufficient conditions for application of a concept. Thus, when one did philosophy of law with a view to conceptual analysis, one asked after the necessary and sufficient conditions for the concept of 'law'. Was this what Hart had in mind when he wrote *The Concept of Law?* There can be little doubt that this question will likely never receive a definitive answer, for there exists evidence for more than one answer to the question. Thus, instead of trying to characterise what Hart did, I will describe his project and the contours of the position he advanced.

Law, Hart argued, is a matter of rules; rules of various kinds, to be sure. But the nerve of law was rules. So-called 'modern' legal systems were comprised of primary and secondary rules. The regime of secondary rules was of vital importance, because it was in the realm of secondary rules that one found the rules for introducing, amending and repealing primary rules. Most importantly, the so-called 'master Secondary Rule' – the Rule of Recognition – was the means by which primary rules were identified as rules of law. The Rule of Recognition, Hart argued, provided both citizen and legal official alike with 'authoritative criteria' for identifying primary rules of obligation.[4] Hart was quick to point out that in modern legal systems, the Rule of Recognition might be quite complex: in short, there might well be multiple 'sources' of law. Owing to its complexity, the Rule of Recognition of virtually any modern legal system is likely to be so complex that it warrants characterization as a 'practice'. Further, Hart indicated quite clearly that the Rule of Recognition

[2] N. Lacey, *A Life of H.L.A. Hart: The Nightmare and the Noble Dream* (Oxford 2004) 112–151.
[3] Hart, *Concept*, vi.
[4] Hart, *Concept*, 94–95.

was ultimate in the chain of validity: the Rule was, itself, neither valid nor invalid. Rather, it was simply 'accepted'.[5]

So far, I have described only one of the two principal parts of *The Concept of Law*. After describing the core features of a municipal legal system, Hart then turned his attention to adjudication. The seventh chapter of *The Concept of Law* introduces themes and questions that remain central to the discussion of Hart's jurisprudence. In terms we would recognise today, Hart begins with questions of rule-following. While Hart treats problems of rule-following from the point of view of both precedent and legislation, he takes an approach that we would instantly recognise as informed by Wittgenstein's problem of rule-following discussed in *Philosophical Investigations.*

Famously, Hart introduces the concept of discretion as the nerve of his account of interpretation. Although Hart has some harsh things to say about rule-scepticism, he concedes that 'a large and important field is left open for the exercise of discretion by the courts and other officials...'.[6] Of course, the role of discretion in Hart's position became a central focus of debate. In *Concept,* Hart limits his discussion of discretion to two aspects: policy implications and the particulars of individual cases. From the vantage point of the present, Hart's discussion of discretion is simple and unsophisticated. In fact, Hart's entire discussion of adjudication is of largely historical interest.

Let us return to the question asked earlier; that is, how to characterise Hart's project in *The Concept of Law*. In describing the contours of a municipal legal system, Hart clearly saw himself as doing abstract work. True, he did say that *The Concept of Law* might possibly be described as a work in 'descriptive sociology'.[7] Whatever one makes of this comment, it is clear that Hart's primary concern was with what he termed 'analysis'. Hart came to jurisprudence with only the Command Theory in view. There was something deeply wrong with this view and Hart spends a fair amount of time in *Concept* getting clear about the shortcomings of the Command Theory and what a proper view of the essential features of law would look like.

1 Raz, Authority and Conceptual Analysis

Contemporary legal positivists can be divided into two groups. The division is driven by differing conceptions of the relationship between law and moral standards. So-called 'inclusive positivists' maintain that legal systems may be worthy of the name 'legal' even though they explicitly incorporate moral standards into law. By contrast, so-called 'exclusive positivists' maintain that no norm can be 'legal' in nature if it incorporates moral notions into the criteria of legal validity. The debate between

[5] Hart, *Concept*, 105–110.
[6] Hart, *Concept*, 136.
[7] Hart, *Concept*, v.

these two positivist camps has come down to a central claim about 'the nature of law'. The burden of proof would seem to lie with the hard positivists, for it is they who are making the strongest claim about the concept of 'law'. The claim is one that sounds in 'necessity'; that is, for a norm to be 'legal' it must possess certain essential features. The most compelling argument for the hard positivist view comes from Joseph Raz, specifically Raz's account of law's authority.

Raz's account of authority is an essential feature of his view of the nature of law. He maintains that the law necessarily claims to be a genuine and not merely *de facto* authority. And for law to fulfil the mediating role that it claims for itself, on Raz's view, the law must issue dictates that can be readily understood and acted upon. More specifically, people need to be able to grasp legal norms (i.e., identify those norms as 'valid') independently of their identifying and considering the (dependent) reasons for those norms. It is for this reason that Raz's position can be characterised as exclusive legal positivism.

Exclusive legal positivists insist that the content of law must come from social sources alone. Raz articulates the 'sources thesis' as follows: 'All law is source based. A law is source-based if its existence and content can be identified by reference to social facts alone, without resort to any evaluative argument'.[8]

Although some read him as making a moral argument,[9] I think it more accurate to read Raz as making a conceptual or metaphysical claim about the nature of law. In this regard, Raz himself has been somewhat equivocal on the matter, sometimes speaking of 'the' concept of authority, 'our' concept of authority or, more recently, 'concept(s) of authority'.[10]

The problem with Raz's position is that he makes no arguments directly in support of his claims for necessity. This is no small omission, for the success of Raz's account of law's authority depends upon the strength of his claim that the concept of law is 'special' in that its meaning is not a function of linguistic usage and, further, that the content of the concept is (at least in part) dictated by something other than conventions for the use of the word.

I believe that Raz needs to answer the question of the nature of law with an account of concepts. To answer the question of the nature of 'law' we need to know what sort of concept law is. Once we have answered what the concept of law is, we can move toward answering what sort of conceptual analysis is necessary for a concept like 'law'. In short, an account of concepts is a necessary preliminary to answering the question 'what is the nature of 'law'?'

The conventional metaphysical wisdom is that concepts divide up into at least two categories: natural kind concepts and artefactual kinds. Natural kind concepts are those whose essence is dictated by a microstructural element such as atomic

---

[8] J. Raz, *Ethics in the Public Domain* (Oxford 1994) 211.

[9] S. R. Perry, 'Hart's Methodological Positivism', in: J.L. Coleman (ed.), *Hart's Postscript* (New York 2001) 311–354.

[10] J. Raz, 'Can There Be a Theory of Law?', in: M. Golding and W. Edmundson (eds.), *The Blackwell Guide to the Philosophy of Law and Legal Theory* (Oxford 2005) 324–42, and 'The Problem of Authority: Revisiting the Service Conception', *Minnesota Law Review* 90.4 (2006), 1003–44.

formula or DNA. Artefactual kinds are the product of human invention. These 'social constructs' are the stuff of John Searle's 'Institutional Facts'[11]: their existence depends upon our attitudes or intentions. Where does Raz's account of the nature of law fall into this divide? It is not at all clear.

On the one hand, Raz says this about the nature of law: 'A theory consists of necessary truths, for only necessary truths about the law reveal the nature of law'.[12] But Raz also maintains that '[i]n large measure what we study when we study the nature of law is the nature of our own self-understanding'.[13] It is difficult to see how necessary truths can arise out of the self-understanding of participants in a practice. Raz seems to want an account of the nature of law that identifies necessary truths; at the same time it identifies something seemingly contingent about law (i.e., our self-understanding of it). Putting together necessity and contingency seems to me to be the next step in the development of exclusive legal positivism. Until Raz accomplishes this task, his claims for law's authority are unconvincing.

2 Dworkinian Constructivism

Dworkin's jurisprudence is both a criticism of and an alternative to all forms of positivism. It is conventional wisdom that positivists believe that the content of law can be identified by a conventional practice Hart dubbed 'the Rule of Recognition'. For positivists, the content of law – or the answer to the question 'What is the law in this jurisdiction?' – is amenable to a descriptive report. Dworkin flatly denies this. In fact, for Dworkin, it is never possible to merely report the state of law on any but the simplest of legal questions because the concept of 'law' is infinitely controversial.

Dworkin's 'interpretive' account of law is grounded in the idea that to understand the concept 'law' one has to identify the point or purpose of law. Because the point or purpose of law is inherently controversial, no account of the law can be merely descriptive. For, any such account will always depend upon a controversial thesis about the point of law, which thesis will drive the selection of some features of the practice and not others. Hence, all accounts of law are necessarily 'constructive' in that their focus on some features of the practice and not others is a matter of selection driven by a prior choice of normative framework (i.e., an account of the 'point' of law).

Dworkin's argument about the need to discern the 'point of law' is driven by his more basic assertion that any conception of law 'must explain how what it takes to be law provides a general justification for the exercise of coercive power by the state'.[14] Hart has never agreed with this characterization of jurisprudence.[15] Some

---

[11] J. Searle, *The construction of social reality* (New York 1995) 31–52.

[12] Raz, *Can There Be a Theory of Law?, 328.*

[13] Raz, *Can There Be a Theory of Law?, 331.*

[14] R. Dworkin, *Law's Empire* (London 1986) 190.

[15] Hart, *Concept*, 239–240.

read Dworkin as asking a different question than Hart and, thus, agree with Hart that Dworkin and he are engaged in fundamentally different projects.[16] This is an uncharitable if not incorrect reading of Dworkin. It is uncharitable in that it fails to take Dworkin's criticism seriously. Dworkin is arguing that Hart assumes away a problem Dworkin maintains is fundamental to any account of law. In other words, Dworkin argues that Hart misunderstands a central feature of his own (i.e., Hart's) account of law. This is not to suggest that Dworkin is correct in his critique of Hart. Rather, it is to suggest that Dworkin has a point, albeit a controversial one.

If we take Dworkin seriously, the question is whether or not he is correct in his claims for the inherently controversial nature of the concept of law. To answer this question, Dworkin needs to advance arguments about the nature of concepts or, at least, some account of why the concept of 'law' is special. Alas, he supplies no arguments to sustain his controversial assertion. And the burden of proof clearly lies with Dworkin. When Hart explicates the Rule of Recognition, he is providing an account of how participants in the practice of law understand judgments of validity. In providing his account of this practice, the measure of Hart's work is accuracy: does Hart's description account for what participants in the practice take to be the central features of validity conditions for law? Dworkin's critique has to be read to claim that even if Hart's account is an accurate sociological account of what participants in the practice take themselves to be doing, that account is not necessarily correct from the point of view of 'law' as it is properly understood.

It seems that, at bottom, Dworkin's debate with Hart is one about the meaning of concepts, more precisely the meaning of the concept of 'law' in the law. Hart says that the meaning of 'law' (its extension) is fixed by what participants in the practice take the concept to mean. Dworkin denies that the way participants understand themselves exhausts the meaning of the concepts they employ. Dworkin (and, interestingly, Raz) maintain that 'law' is a concept the content of which is (in part) dictated by something other than conventional understanding. How do we understand this?

3 Two Approaches to Practice

Hart and Dworkin disagree about the role of practice in theory. For Dworkin, practice is material that is taken up by a theory. It is fuel or content. For Hart, practice is the product of history and cannot be 'theorised'. The Rule of Recognition cannot be theoretically justified because it is a product of history and circumstance. Dworkin cannot abide this quietism. In terms that are all too familiar, it can be said that

[16] B. Leiter, 'Beyond the Hart/Dworkin Debate: The Methodology Problem in Jurisprudence', *American Journal of Jurisprudence* 48.1 (2003), 17–51.

Dworkin privileges 'theory' over practice.[17] For Hart, it is always practice which is primary.

Dworkin clearly believes that theory is the preferred route to a better understanding of the practice of law. As others have argued, this claim is wildly implausible.[18] Dworkin is ultimately not interested in an account of law as we find it (in practice). Rather, his project is devoted to providing us with an ideal conception of law, the merits of which are not discernible by the degree to which the theorising illuminates the practice to which it is purportedly directed.

By contrast, Hart explores the social dimensions of legal practice, rooting his positivism in the critical, reflective attitudes of institutional participants in law. As mentioned earlier, the principal elements of Hart's account are the concepts of primary and secondary rules, the internal point of view, and, most importantly, the Rule of Recognition. Through the use of the Rule of Recognition, lawyers and non-lawyers alike are able to identify legal norms and in that way, decide what the law is on any given question.

There can be little doubt that Hart provides the contours of a 'practice theory' approach to law. By 'practice theory,' I mean an account of law that answers the question 'What is the law in this jurisdiction with respect to *x*?' by looking at how participants in the practice decide the state of the law. Hart gave us only the barest essentials in outlining the Rule of Recognition.[19] To be sure, he made it clear that

---

[17] Ronald Dworkin himself says as much. See R. Dworkin, *Justice in Robes* (Cambridge 2006) 170. 'We understand legal practice better, and make more intelligible sense of propositions of law, by pursuing an explicitly normative and political enterprise: refining, and defending conceptions of legality and drawing tests for concrete claims of law from favored conceptions. There is no question of taking theories of law constructed in that way to be merely "descriptive". They are conceptual, but only in the normative, interpretive sense in which theories of justice, as well as theories of democracy, liberty, and equality are conceptual.'

[18] See, e.g., B. Leiter, 'The Theory of Esoteric Law' *The Journal of Legal Education,* Summer (2007) (reviewing) *Ronald Dworkin, Justice in Robes* and Scott Hershovitz (ed.), *Exploring Law's Empire: The Jurisprudence of Ronald Dworkin* (Oxford 2006). Leiter writes:

> 'Readers of *Law's Empire* had long thought that Dworkin had not given us an account of the concept of *law* in competition with Hart's, but rather an account of *ideal law,* of what the law "ought to be" if it realised the many virtues we associate with the "rule of law" – what, in a word, Dworkin calls "integrity". Dworkin's rejoinder to Hart's "Postscript" now effectively concedes the point. Dworkin tells us that he is really interested in an analysis of the concept of "legality" or the "rule of law", a necessarily evaluative inquiry'.

[19] Coleman comments that while Hart himself 'occasionally' identified the Rule of Recognition as 'a social practice,' Coleman thinks this view mistaken. He writes:

> '...the two [ie, the Rule of Recognition and a social practice] cannot possibly be the same thing. The rule of recognition is a rule, and, thus an abstract, propositional entity. The practice is constituted in part by behaviour, and is thus not a propositional entity. The rule has conditions of satisfaction; the practice does not. If the rule is not identical with the practice, what is the relationship between them?'

J. Coleman, The Practice of Principle: In Defense of a Pragmatist Approach to Legal Theory (Oxford 2003) 77–78.

[the] Rule of Recognition is a practice, one that lies at the heart of Hart's account of law as a practice of special social rules.[20] But what do we mean when we say that law is a 'practice,' albeit one of a special sort? For answer to that question, let us turn to the literature on practices.

4 Practice Theory

When theorising a human activity, one of the most fundamental questions is locating the vantage point from which to start the endeavour. Consider the philosophy of mind. Cognitive naturalists of a variety of orientations (Fodor, Chomsky, Searle, the Churchlands and Dennett) argue that problems of mind and consciousness are best explained by investigation of the inner theatre of mind or brain. For them, philosophy of mind is a matter of theorising the relationship between mental activity and our efforts to represent reality outside the mind. By contrast, non-naturalists like Sellars, Davidson, McDowell and Brandom follow Wittgenstein in seeing mind not as a thing or a place but as an array of social skills and activities. For the non-naturalists, 'practices' are the places where 'the mind' is on display. An account of the skills necessary to participate in practices are the non-naturalists' account of 'mind'. Importantly the non-naturalists can theorise mind as found in practices without resort to the inner theatre that preoccupies the naturalists.[21]

As a point of philosophical focus, practice theory ranges across a wide variety of social activities and philosophical specialties. As Joseph Rouse explains in his recent overview of practice theory,[22] the role of language in social practices has been a particular focus of attention for philosophers. One prominent example that has made its way into the legal literature[23] is Robert Brandom's inferentialist account of the normativity of practices. Like other non-naturalists, Brandom is keen to provide an account of normativity in practices that locates the explanatory power of the account in linguistic utterances/exchanges between participants in discursive practices.

In his account of practice theory, Rouse identifies six principal features of practice theory that make it a central theme in social theory, social science and philosophy. The first of these is Practices, Rules and Norms. Here Rouse singles out Wittgenstein and Heidegger as central figures in the development of the idea that

---

[20] I think there is a great deal more to be said about the Rule of Recognition. Specifically, we want to know precisely how the practice that Hart identifies as the Rule of Recognition provides the tools for appraising claims about the law of a particular jurisdiction.

[21] An overview of the naturalist/non-naturalist debate in the philosophy of mind is found in R. Rorty, 'Naturalism and Quietism,' in Richard Rorty, *Philosophical Papers Vol. 4: Philosophy as Cultural Politics* (Cambridge 2007) 147–159.

[22] J. Rouse, 'Practice Theory' in S.P. Turner and M.W. Risjord (eds.), *Handbook of the Philosophy of Science* (Amsterdam 2006).

[23] See D. Canale and T. Giovanni, 'On Legal Inferentialism: Toward a Pragmatics of Semantic Content in Legal Interpretation'20 *Ratio Juris* (2007), 32–44.

normativity arises from social practices. Wittgenstein's rule-following arguments and Heidegger's account of the relationship between understanding and interpretation locate normativity in social interactions in ongoing practices. In the hands of someone like Charles Taylor, the Wittgenstein-Heidegger account of normativity shows how a naturalist account of human behaviour fails to capture its essential features. Identifications of our behaviour in terms of 'brute data' fail to illuminate the intentionality that underwrites our collective interactions. It is our practices that give rules and norms their meaning and, hence, their authoritative status in our practices.

The second theme Rouse explores is the relationship between practices and individual agency. The question here is that of the proper ontological focus of philosophical theorising. The central issue is whether practices can be explained at the level of the whole or whether individual action can be rendered intelligible apart from the social or cultural context.

One way of tackling this problem is provided by Stephen Turner in the form of a puzzle. Turner writes:

> We often cannot understand what other people mean other than by translation.... [and] often cannot understand what the behaviour, gesture and doings of other people mean other than by consciously inventing and then selecting on the basis of observation a hypothesis that explains this behaviour. But we know that the people we are attempting to understand did not themselves acquire their capacity to speak a language through formal teaching or books, or come to understand one another's gestures and performances by consciously constructing and testing hypotheses. So there must be some way to acquire [these] capacities. The puzzle is how they are acquired.[24]

The puzzle is one about the relationship between time and iterability. Practices change over time. Yet, the changes can only occur through the actions of participants. But if the actions of participants are determined by the practice (i.e., the practice 'constitutes' individual action) then the role of individual agency in the transformation of practices remains a mystery. As Rouse comments:

> If practices are temporally extended patterns of activity by multiple agents (perhaps encompassing more than one generation of practitioners), then the question of how this pattern is sustained, transmitted, and imposed upon subsequent performances has to be a primary theoretical concern.[25]

Bodily skills and disciplines form the third focus of Rouse's themes of the practice theory literature. The connection between the body and skills is but another opportunity to assess the role of causation in the explanation of human action. The question is the degree to which behaviour or action can be explained by causal forces? That is, are our 'doings' explicable in the language of causes or is there are irreducibly social component to human action? It is the realization of human agency in practices that makes isolation of causal forces difficult to achieve. Thus, theorists such as Hubert Dreyfus maintain that while initiation into a practice can

---

[24] S. Turner, *The Social Theory of Practices: Tradition, Tacit Knowledge and Presuppositions* (Chicago 1994) 46.
[25] Rouse, *Practice Theory*, 647.

be explained in causal terms, the causal narrative loses its efficacy as the agent is integrated into the practice.[26]

In explaining the role of action in practices, we might say that there are both surface and depth dimensions to action. The idea of a 'depth explanation' is best captured by Michael Polanyi's phrase 'tacit knowledge'. Kuhn's scientist, working under conditions of normal science, works within a 'paradigm' that serves as the backdrop for research. The commitments, presuppositions and assumptions of the scientist serve as the background against which the scientific endeavour is pursued.[27] In this regard, one question for practice theorists is whether there is a cognitive dimension to this background? Can the background be explicated and described and do they really account for what we take to be 'scientific knowledge'?

When we consider a practice such as law, the notion of 'shared presuppositions' is easily understood and, yet, potentially controversial. Consider Hart's claims about the Rule of Recognition.[28] The Rule of Recognition provides criteria for distinguishing valid from spurious law. But the Rule of Recognition is neither valid nor invalid. More importantly, its criteria are shared through practice and validated in use. What clearer example of 'tacit assumptions' could one find?[29]

But what problem does the idea of shared, tacit presuppositions solve? Rouse points out that in his account of scientific practice, Kuhn uses the presuppositions attaching to different research paradigms as a way of explaining how scientists talk past one another.[30] Would such an idea explain why positivists and interpretivists often seem to speak past one another? It might.

---

[26] See generally H. Dreyfus, *What Computers Can't Do: The Limits of Artificial Intelligence* (New York 1979); H. Dreyfus, *Being-in-the-World: A Commentary on Heidegger's Being and Time* (Cambridge, Mass. 1991).

[27] Rouse comments:

> These themes became especially prominent through their emergence in the philosophy of natural science from the late 1950's through the 1970's. Against the prevailing logical empiricist claim that the norms of scientific reasoning could be expressed as purely formal, logical principles that any rational human being should endorse, Kuhn, Toulmin, Feyerabend, Polanyi, and Hanson and others argued that substantive commitments shared by scientific communities played an ineliminable role in actual scientific reasoning. Many practice theorists concluded that if even the natural sciences, an apparent exemplar of rationality, rely upon prior unarticulated commitments, then surely other areas of human activity do likewise.

Rouse, *Practice Theory,* 656 (citations omitted).

[28] Hart, *Concept*, 94–95.

[29] Of course, Dworkinians contest the very existence of a Rule of Recognition. Their claim is not theoretical but empirical: no such rule exists, tacitly or otherwise.

[30] Kuhn writes:

> To translate a theory or worldview into one's own language is not to make it one's own. For that one must go native, discover that one is thinking and working in, not simply translating out of, a language that was previously foreign. That transition is not, however, one that an individual may make or refrain from making by deliberation and choice… [Instead] he finds he has slipped into the new language without a decision having been made.

T. Kuhn, *The Structure of Scientific Revolutions*, 2nd edition (Chicago 1970) 204.

Can practices be the object of scientific inquiry? With the appearance of naturalism on the jurisprudential scene,[31] this consideration – the penultimate in Rouse's list of six – becomes important. Scientific explanation is explanation by appeal to causal laws. Are human practices such as gift giving, friendship or law amenable to explanation by appeal to causal laws? Alasdair MacIntyre and Polanyi both argue that social practices are unpredictable in ways that elude the explanatory rigor of science. Hermeneutic practice theorists take this idea further, arguing that the only way to make sense of practices is through a process of continuing 'interpretation'.

Rouse's final expository theme is the disciplinary autonomy of practices. The question here is whether the social context can be reduced to another vocabulary? A reductivist enterprise familiar to lawyers is economics. Economics 'make sense' of tort law on the model of efficiency. 'Efficiency' answers the question 'What is the point of tort law?' or 'Why does tort law exist?' The language of economics replaces the normative language of law in that the vocabulary of economics is shown to be more basic and, so economics argue, capable of unearthing the 'real' reasons why we have tort law.

But Jules Coleman has shown that, at least as a conceptual account of tort law, economics fails miserably.[32] Nothing can count as an explanation of a practice that fails to illuminate what the participants take to be central features of the practice. In Coleman's view, economic analysis 'renders the structure of tort law mysterious; it suggests a scheme of practical inference altogether different from the one actually in place; and its reductionist impulse leads the economist to jettison concepts that are in fact central to our legal practice'.[33]

5 Regulism and Normativity

The most important aspect of any account of law as a practice is explicating the role played by 'normativity'. Robert Brandom's discussion of 'regulism' provides an entry into the problem of normativity and its role in practices. To be clear, what we are after is an account of norms that illuminates the connection between norms and reasons. Along the way, we will have things to say about naturalism and intentionality, just to name two related topics. But the central focus is the role of normativity in practices.

When is a performance correct? In virtue of what is it true to say 'she did it right'? Brandom begins his answer by reminding us that for Kant, 'what makes a performance correct or not is its relation to some explicit rule'.[34] But what is the Kantian conception of 'performance in accordance with an explicit rule'? Brandom answers: 'to assess correctness is always to make at least implicit reference to a rule

[31] See, e.g., B. Leiter, *Naturalizing Jurisprudence* (Oxford 2007).

[32] See Coleman, *Practice of principle*.

[33] Coleman, *Practice of principle*, 23.

[34] R.B. Brandom, *Making It Explicit: Reasoning, Representing and Discursive Commitment* (Harvard 1994) 18–19.

or principle that *determines* what is correct by explicitly *saying* so'.[35] The rule and nothing but the rule determines what counts as 'correct' in following the rule. The norm sets out its own standards of correctness. There is nothing between the rule and what counts as complying with it.

In a move that is now common, Brandom uses Wittgenstein's regress argument to show that the Kantian, regulist account of norms renders them unintelligible.[36] According to Brandom, Wittgenstein's regress argument is his 'master argument for the appropriateness of the pragmatist rather than the regulist/intellectualist, order of explanation'.[37] On a pragmatist conception of norms, a conception of correctness of performance is implicit in practice.[38] Practice is the ground of normativity for practice is the means by which the regress argument is answered and the problems of regulism avoided.

But what account of practice is appropriate? Rouse has recently added depth to Brandom's arguments in ways that may prove useful to legal philosophers. As Brandom argues, 'being in a practice' is all about mutual accountability. Maintenance of a practice is achieved through iteration of performances that require mutual accountability on the part of participants in the practice. But how is this achieved? Rouse suggests this as a test: 'a performance belongs to a practice if it is appropriate to hold it accountable as a correct or incorrect performance of that practice'.[39] Fleshing out this general conception of accountability is the first step to developing a convincing account of the normativity of practices.

First, we demarcate practices from one another by the 'ways in which constitutive performances bear on one another'.[40] So, performances respond to one another through correction, praise, explication and drawing inferences. Brandom's own account of normativity as 'deontic scorekeeping' is but one example of how this notion of a practice as an interactive field of performance can be explicated.

Rouse argues for a second feature of a practice conceived as a 'network of mutually interactive performances' and that is the requirement 'that these patterns of interaction constitute something at issue and at stake in their outcomes'.[41] Core or recurrent questions are but one illustration of what gives a practice and its performances their identifiable character. Again, Brandom explicates this well:

> Each perspective is at most locally privileged in that it incorporates a structural distinction between objectively correct applications of concepts and applications that are merely subjectively taken to be correct. But none of these perspectives is privileged in advance over any other.... Sorting out who should be counted as correct, whose claims and applications of concepts should be treated as authoritative, is a messy retail business.... [T]here is no

[35] Brandom, *Making it Explicit*, 20. Brandom characterises this conception of norms as 'Platonist' and he sees it as 'common to Kant and Frege'.
[36] Brandom, *Making it Explicit*, 21.
[37] Brandom, *Making it Explicit*, 23.
[38] Brandom, *Making it Explicit*, 21.
[39] J. Rouse, 'Social Practices and Normativity' 37 *Philosophy of the Social Sciences* (2007), 46, 48.
[40] Rouse, *Social Practices and Normativity*, 49.
[41] Rouse, *Social Practices and Normativity*, 50.

> bird's-eye view above the fray of competing claims from which those that deserve to prevail can be identified. . . .[42]

Time is a crucial aspect of this account of the normativity of practices. The unity that makes the practice more than just a series of (unrelated) actions over time is that the performances are directed to one another *over time*.[43] It is the return of participants to recurrent issues and questions, addressed in the same way, that demarcates one practice from another.

6 Normativity and the Practice of Law

The goal of any practice account of law has to be making sense of the practice as an ongoing, iterative and, most importantly, common activity. In providing an account of normativity, it is crucial that any account of law as a practice illuminates precisely how participants can be said to perform in a common world. What is it that makes the world 'common'? And when participants disagree about their purportedly common world, how are such disagreements framed and adjudicated?

In what remains the definitive critique of interpretivism, Gerald Postema provided the first detailed outline of a practice theory of law.[44] The first place to begin is explication of what Postema calls 'the common world'. What joins lawyers together in a common practice? Beliefs; propositional attitudes; intentionality; forms of argument, or consensus in judgment. One or all of these candidates is likely efficacious as a ground of any analysis of law as a practice.[45]

Second is the question of consensus. Do participants share a practice if they share only questions about the nature of the practice? Dworkin famously argues that mere questions alone (e.g., about the grounds of law) suffice to bring performers together in the 'same' practice. Postema makes a strong case in the proposition that disagreement is possible only against the background of deep shared commitments. His argument is persuasive but it is just a start.

An effective account of law as a practice will answer the interpretivist question about the grounds of law. As Postema argues convincingly, the unity and coherence of law does not depend on a structure of rules nor a regime of principles. What, then does this unity consist in? The answer to this question is for another day.

---

[42] Brandom, *Making it Explicit*, 600–601.

[43] A brilliant discussion of this point is found in Meredith Williams, *Wittgenstein, Mind and Meaning: Toward a Social Conception of Mind* (London 1999) 169. ('The normativity of rules is grounded in community agreement over time. . . '.)

[44] G. Postema, 'Protestant Interpretation and Social Practice' 6 *Law and Philosophy* (1987) 283.

[45] It remains to be seen just what emerges as the focus for of explication in rendering 'the common element' in law intelligible. This article is but a tentative first step in identifying the issues and questions that need to be addressed if a practice theory account of law is to be a fruitful research path.

FSC
www.fsc.org
MIX
Papier | Fördert
gute Waldnutzung
FSC® C083411

Kolibri 360 GmbH
Ferdinand-Jühlke-Straße 7
99095 Erfurt, Deutschland
produktsicherheit@kolibri360.de